Effective Planned Change Strategies

G. Melvin Hipps, *Editor*

NEW DIRECTIONS FOR INSTITUTIONAL RESEARCH
Sponsored by the Association for Institutional Research
MARVIN W. PETERSON, *Editor-in-Chief*

Number 33, March 1982

Paperback sourcebooks in
The Jossey-Bass Higher Education Series

Jossey-Bass Inc., Publishers
San Francisco • Washington • London

Effective Planned Change Strategies
Volume IX, Number 1, March 1982
G. Melvin Hipps, *Editor*

New Directions for Institutional Research Series
Marvin W. Peterson, *Editor-in-Chief*

Copyright © 1982 by Jossey-Bass Inc., Publishers
and
Jossey-Bass Limited

Copyright under International, Pan American, and Universal
Copyright Conventions. All rights reserved. No part of
this issue may be reproduced in any form—except for brief
quotation (not to exceed 500 words) in a review or professional
work—without permission in writing from the publishers.

New Directions for Institutional Research (publication number
USPS 098-830) is published quarterly by Jossey-Bass Inc.,
Publishers, and is sponsored by the Association for Institutional
Research. The volume and issue numbers above are included for
the convenience of libraries. Second-class postage rates paid at
San Francisco, California, and at additional mailing offices.

Correspondence:
Subscriptions, single-issue orders, change of address notices,
undelivered copies, and other correspondence should be sent to
New Directions Subscriptions, Jossey-Bass Inc., Publishers,
433 California Street, San Francisco, California 94104.

Editorial correspondence should be sent to the Editor-in-Chief,
Marvin W. Peterson, Center for the Study of Higher Education,
University of Michigan, Ann Arbor, Michigan 48109.

Library of Congress Catalogue Card Number LC 81-48481
International Standard Serial Number ISSN 0271-0579
International Standard Book Number ISBN 87589-903-X

Cover art by Willi Baum
Manufactured in the United States of America

Ordering Information

The paperback sourcebooks listed below are published quarterly and can be ordered either by subscription or as single copies.

Subscriptions cost $35.00 per year for institutions, agencies, and libraries. Individuals can subscribe at the special rate of $21.00 per year *if payment is by personal check.* (Note that the full rate of $35.00 applies if payment is by institutional check, even if the subscription is designated for an individual.) Standing orders are accepted.

Single copies are available at $7.95 when payment accompanies order, and *all single-copy orders under $25.00 must include payment.* (California, Washington, D.C., New Jersey, and New York residents please include appropriate sales tax.) For billed orders, cost per copy is $7.95 plus postage and handling. (Prices subject to change without notice.)

To ensure correct and prompt delivery, all orders must give either the *name of an individual* or an *official purchase order number.* Please submit your order as follows:

Subscriptions: specify series and subscription year.
Single Copies: specify sourcebook code and issue number (such as, IR8).

Mail orders for United States and Possessions, Latin America, Canada, Japan, Australia, and New Zealand to:
  Jossey-Bass Inc., Publishers
  433 California Street
  San Francisco, California 94104

Mail orders for all other parts of the world to:
  Jossey-Bass Limited
  28 Banner Street
  London EC1Y 8QE

New Directions for Institutional Research Series
Marvin W. Peterson, *Editor-in-Chief*

Contents

Chapter 1. Changes in Higher Education: Forces and Impacts   **5**
Donald D. Christenson

The changing environment of higher education (economic conditions, students, the world of work) are making and will continue to make significant impacts on higher education systems, educational programs, student services, faculty, and governance of colleges and universities. Institutions can reduce the negative consequences of these impacts by anticipating changes and planning strategies to deal with them.

Chapter 2. Planned Change in Institutions of   **19**
Higher Learning
Philip C. Winstead

Colleges and universities can enhance their effectiveness by adopting a systems approach to organizing, planning, decision making, and evaluating. One model that exemplifies this approach is a decentralized, participative one that emphasizes systematic planning and management by objectives.

Chapter 3. Team Leadership Development   **33**
Velma Pomrenke

Many of the problems faced by a college or university can be solved effectively by groups or teams if individuals who make up the teams are given the leadership and collaborative skills necessary for productive teamwork.

Chapter 4. Faculty and Administrative Development   **49**
G. Melvin Hipps

A comprehensive faculty and administrative development program involves instructional development, curricular development, organizational development, personal development, and professional development.

Chapter 5. Case Study: The University of Akron Experience   **67**
Foster S. Buchtel

Planned change can be effected by (1) involving a broad cross section of a university community in discussions of the problems faced by the institution and the opportunities available for solving these problems; (2) providing training in interpersonal relationships and group dynamics and knowledge about university organizations and environmental influences on higher education; (3) organizing task forces to study and recommend solutions to problems; and (4) setting up interdisciplinary/interdepartmental internships to establish a faculty/administrative team leadership development program.

The Association for Institutional Research was created in 1966 to benefit, assist, and advance research leading to improved understanding, planning, and operation of institutions of higher education. Publication policy is set by its Publications Board.

Foreword

The ultimate goal of private foundations should be to stimulate and assist individuals, or, frequently, institutions that serve them, to live a more meaningful and rewarding life. Many of the activities assisted by foundations involve this process of personal or institutional improvement. A strategy frequently employed by the W. K. Kellogg Foundation is to provide developmental funds that enable a service agency— such as a hospital, social agency, or university—to mount a new but untried venture, with the promise of a major breakthrough and demonstration of a better way to carry out its mission. Assistance to The University of Akron, Furman University, and Wichita State University to help them increase their leadership and managerial capability, each with its own unique approach, was in this foundation programming tradition.

The common focus on the *process* of change has given the three projects discussed in this sourcebook a special meaning as models to be studied, not necessarily to be emulated, but from which one can learn appropriate applications. Each institution has experiences that provide insights and directions for other similar institutions in building their own approach to planned change.

The three pilot institutions addressed such broad concerns as the context, process, and strategies involved in planned change and the more specific aspects of team leadership development and faculty and administrative development. Most importantly, the narrative that follows is about real events and real people. A theoretical base is provided, but the lessons learned, both positive and negative, are from a context of recent practical experience. The three projects supported by the foundation effectively demonstrated that a generalized model is possible as well as practical for institutions to address common problems such as increasingly limited resources, greater demands for accountability, major shifts in enrollment patterns, and low staff turnover.

The Furman University effort dealt with faculty development and academic planning as one approach to institutional self-renewal. The University of Akron developed a leadership "pool" of faculty and administrators prepared through in-service training to exercise their responsibilities to the change process. Wichita State University

1

brought together trustees, key administrators, faculty, and staff on a series of task forces to develop a university mission and goals statement and through this process refined university team management skills. In all instances there are instructive applications of the concept of planned change.

A careful reading of this publication should provide a series of guidelines and checkpoints. It is meant as a reference and desk manual, not as a blueprint. Typical of the kinds of basic observations that have emanated from the practical experiences of these projects is the straightforward statement found in Chapter Four: "A plan for a faculty and administrative development program is meaningless unless it exists within the framework of institutional development. Therefore, institutions that do not have a scheme for institutional planning are not yet ready to set up a professional development program. One may institute a series of workshops or seminars, but these do not constitute a program."

The Kellogg Foundation tries to ensure that what is learned in the course of developing a successful pilot project is widely known and utilized by other institutions. It is in that spirit that this publication is offered. The ultimate evaluation of this endeavor and subsequent efforts to make use of the insights developed from the three approaches to planned change will come far in the future. The worth of this, and other dissemination and utilization activities, will be reflected in the extent to which the concepts set forth in the following pages improve the educational enterprise and quality of education provided students at utilizing institutions.

Robert E. Kinsinger
Vice-President
W. K. Kellogg Foundation

Editor's Notes

During the latter part of the decade of the 1970s, The University of Akron, Furman University, and Wichita State University undertook programs of planned change that they hoped would allow them not only to survive during the period of retrenchment in higher education but to improve the quality of their academic programs and of their service to the larger communities of which they are a part. Portions of their programs for planned change were supported by grants from the W. K. Kellogg Foundation. Officials at the Foundation felt that the ideas generated in these projects could be of some help to other institutions that were attempting to manage the process of change and thus agreed to support a national dissemination project of which this monograph was a part.

The first four chapters of this sourcebook present the environmental and theoretical frameworks in which the projects at the three universities took place and in which the authors believe any institutional effort to bring about change must take place. Chapters Five, Six, and Seven are case studies which detail the planning, implementation, and evaluation of the program at each university.

Chapter Eight summarizes the three projects and analyzes eight elements common to all three of them. These constitute whatever generalizable model that might be derived from the three programs. Chapter Nine is an epilogue in which Marvin W. Peterson presents an assessment of the value of the projects, discusses some elements of change theory demonstrated by the projects, and speculates about the future of these programs and other similiar programs.

G. Melvin Hipps
Editor

This sourcebook has been produced as a part of a project to disseminate the ideas concerning planned change developed by The University of Akron, Furman University, and Wichita State University through programs supported by grants from the W. K. Kellogg Foundation.

4

G. Melvin Hipps, currently a writer and consultant in higher education, was formerly professor of education and English, associate academic dean, chairman, Department of Education, director of Graduate Studies, and coordinator of Programs for Faculty Development at Furman University. He was codirector of the Kellogg-sponsored project at Furman.

Each university must analyze its own situation, the forces of change in motion within its own environment, and the special implications of the changes.

Changes in Higher Education: Forces and Impacts

Donald D. Christenson

The changes that will occur in the environment of higher education during the 1980s cannot be predicted with ease and complete accuracy. Despite the difficulties, it is necessary to try to predict the future and to plan for it. Colleges and universities must identify the forces that affect them, speculate on the changes that will occur, trace backward from the future to the present the implications of the changes, and then plan what actions they will take to address the future they have hypothesized. The value of this exercise is not simply the final plan, but the process itself. The process involves a different way of thinking from the traditional approach of projecting the past into the future in a linear manner.

The pressures faced by higher education are complex and contradictory. On the one hand, society demands that colleges and universities take a larger, more diverse role in contemporary American life. On the other hand, leveling enrollments, the realities of political power, and the relative scarcity of financial and other resources have seriously restricted their ability to preserve the best of the past while simultaneously striking out in new directions.

G. Hipps (Ed.). *New Directions for Institutional Research: Effective Planned Change Strategies*, no. 33. San Francisco: Jossey-Bass, March 1982.

Higher education has entered a period of limited growth that is projected to extend into the 1990s. There are, however, opportunities for those institutions that anticipate the changing forces and develop appropriate responses. The concerns, objectives, and criteria for success will shift from growth to quality. Postsecondary institutions in the next decade will have to discover how to emphasize the quality of what they do with the relatively fixed resources. When a positive approach to life under conditions of limited growth is identified and accepted, it is not so threatening, and reactions can be more than simply defensive.

Changing Environment of Higher Education

The environment of higher education poses the problems and threats that must be addressed, it offers the potentialities and opportunities for new approaches for those who see and seize them, and it provides the setting within which decisions concerning everything from the nature of the university to day-to-day operations will be made. There is a need, then, systematically to identify which elements of the environment are especially pertinent to higher education, to project the changes that will be occurring in those important elements, and to analyze the implications of the changes for higher education.

Changes in the Environment at Large. Beyond the immediate environment of higher education (students, resources, and so forth) is the broader social, economic, and cultural setting that is the source of most of the basic forces that affect the world of higher education. Many different futurists have identified the major forces they think are shaping our destiny and have speculated on the changes that may occur during the next twenty years. Although writers disagree on the relative significance of the changes, some important forces in our environment are the following ones: the worldwide scarcity and rising cost of the "basics" of food, shelter, and health care; the shifts in population between urban and rural areas and from northern to sunbelt states; the changing life-styles and values; the complexity and unresponsiveness of institutions — government, education, corporations, and labor; the energy crisis; the problem of pollution; the advances in technology; and the population explosion in underdeveloped countries. The potential impact of these environmental factors on colleges and universities is as obvious as it is profound.

Changes in Students. One of the most significant factors in the immediate environment of higher education is the number of potential students, the types of students available, and their patterns of attendance at college. The number of college-age students is decreasing and will continue to decrease by another 20 percent for at least fifteen more years. There is also a decline in the percentage of eighteen-year-olds who are going to college. The relatively stable enrollment figures for the past five years are due to increases in the number of women, minorities, older students, and part-time students. Large numbers of high school graduates are delaying their entry into college for one or more years. Finally, the practice of noncontinuous, in-and-out attendance at college is increasing.

Changes in Education and Work. The forces of change in the world of work are as great as in the world of higher education. The number of jobs, the kinds of jobs available, the kinds of people who work, and the patterns of working are all changing. Work has an effect on the number of people who pursue degrees, the kind of education they want, and their subsequent needs for continuing education.

Since 1975, there has been slower growth in jobs requiring higher education. By 1990, 22 percent of the labor force will have a college degree, compared to 7 percent in 1950. Based on trends, a surplus of 140,000 college graduates each year is projected by 1985 (Johansen and Samuel, 1977). The shift in popularity of the various fields of study is another change brought about by the changes in the world of work. In order to compete in the increasingly tight job market, more students are seeking work in professional and technical fields. The jarring effects of shifting resources to growth fields while others are declining are well known to many universities. The pressures of holding present jobs or moving up create a demand for career-oriented continuing education programs. Thus, more people are returning to take up-to-date advanced specialized work in their original field or to develop a new, complementary field of expertise.

There is also a change in the nature of the work force. For example, the percentage of women participating in the labor forces has increased from about 30 to 45 percent from 1950 to 1975 and could increase to 55 percent by 1990. More people, especially women and older people, are interested in part-time work, and employers' attitudes toward part-time work are changing.

If finding a job will be hard in 1990, getting a promotion will be even more difficult. The 25 to 45 age group (the "baby boom") will comprise 52 percent of the labor force, and the ratio of younger workers to senior workers will increase sharply (Morrison, 1976). The "promotion squeeze," along with changes in basic attitudes, could result in an increase in second careers. Retirement patterns, whether early retirement or delayed retirement, will also affect the nature of the work force.

Changes in Resources. Increases in financial resources for higher education are leveling off. During the growth years of the 1960s, income increased 33 percent, while inflation was running 4 to 6 percent per year. In recent years, state appropriations to higher education have been increasing 12 percent per year (Millett, 1977). Inflation, however, has ranged from 8 percent to an unprecedented 18 percent in the first quarter of 1980. When inflation is escalating, the dilemma for colleges and universities is doubled (Kreps, 1974). The higher education price index has increased from a base of 100 in 1967 to 136 in 1971 to 217 in 1978 (*Chronicle,* September 24, 1979). Prices more than doubled, taking away almost 70 percent of the increase in funds during this period.

The major sources of funds for universities and colleges are the federal and state governments, tuition, and private contributions. In the early 1970s, about 33 percent came from state and local governments, 25 percent from the federal government, 20 percent from tuition, and the remaining 20 percent from auxiliary operations and private gifts (Stewart and Harvey, 1975). Changes worth noting are occurring in each of the major sources of support for universities.

Major federal support has gone to student financial aid and to research. Federal support increased from under $1 billion in 1960 to almost $8 billion in 1975 but has leveled off in the latter 1970s (*Chronicle,* October 9, 1979). States have provided the basic support for faculty, buildings, and operating expenses. State appropriations increased from $6.2 to $19.1 billion from 1969 to 1979. Several forces limit the potential growth of state and federal support. The tax base for many states is limited, and the saturation point in tax rates is being reached as citizens become more resistant to tax increases. The proportion of tax resources going to higher education is stabilizing due to the stabilization of enrollments and the emergence of new priorities for tax support (Didham and others, 1976).

Tuition has been going up at a faster rate than the other sources of support. The rate at which tuition can be increased as a source of additional funding is limited, however, by the effects increases will have on access to education and to enrollments. Private gifts more than doubled in the 1960s. Similarly, endowment funds and the income from endowments more than doubled (Didham and others, 1976). But just as with tax support and tuition, the rate of growth in private gifts has leveled off. There may, however, be factors that are favorable to future increases. The number of alumni has increased substantially in the past twenty years, since a larger percentage of all degrees was awarded during this period. Furthermore, corporations may be increasingly willing to provide educational costs and leaves to their employees for continuing education, and they could also be a sources of applied research funds.

Impacts and Implications of Changes

The changing environment will affect the entire system of higher education, the educational programs, student programs, faculties, and governance and administration of universities and colleges. Although the effects cannot be predicted with certainty, analysis and speculation will at least identify some of the possibilities. Knowing the range of things that could happen provides a better basis for facing the future and preparing for it.

Higher Education System. The entire higher education system will feel the forces of change. The missions of individual institutions, the ways in which institutions compete with and relate to one another, and the level of quality throughout higher education will all feel the effects. Competition will increase, both between different groups of institutions and directly between specific institutions. Since resources are tied largely to student enrollments, institutions will fight to maintain their enrollments so that they will not have to face cuts in resources, programs, and faculty.

Competition has both beneficial and destructive elements. It can, on the one hand, bring higher education to a greater number of qualified people, make higher education more responsive to legitimate societal needs, and enhance sharpness and vitality within the universities. On the other hand, competition can result in lowering quality of students and programs and in divisive, dysfunctional behaviors within the university.

The great growth period in higher education was concerned primarily with quantitative growth. Now, as growth in numbers of students and resources levels off, questions of quality are being increasingly raised (Didham and others, 1976). The concerns about quality relate primarily to students, programs, and faculty. The effects of limited resources and increased competition on quality in higher education are complex and sometimes contradictory. A reduced applicant pool may result in a larger number of unqualified or marginally qualified students. However, more women and older students may be recruited; and these students may be of a higher quality in terms of achievement, ability, and motivation. Some programs may be cut, thus limiting choices for students; however, judicious pruning of the curriculum may enhance an institution's strengths and minimize or eliminate its weak areas. Lower faculty salaries may discourage able teachers from joining or remaining in the profession, but then there is now a large pool of well-qualified faculty that will allow for more selective recruitment.

Beyond increased competition and potential negative impacts on quality, limited resources may also lead to two other consequences: greater coordination and centralization within higher education and greater differentiation between institutions. The purposes of coordination and centralization are to contain destructive competition, to develop a better base of information to use in making tough decisions, and to use more wisely the scarce resources available within a state. Examples of coordination and centralization are the emergence of various types of consortia and the formulation of statewide master plans for higher education. The use of such devices, however, may result in the institution having less flexibility in starting new, innovative programs.

A basic alternative to competing in all directions by "being all things to all people" is to develop a distinctiveness based on the institution's special strengths and unique opportunities. By choosing its own unique role and mission, a university can shield itself from the full force of competition. Efforts to develop statements of role and mission have had a resurgence on many campuses in recent years. Most statements, however, are barely distinguishable from one another, reflecting the reluctance to take the risks involved in charting a distinctive role.

Educational Programs. The educational programs of colleges and universities will be significantly affected by the changes occurring in higher education. There will be constraints on new programs and possible reductions in present programs. Equally important are the surging changes in fields of study. A counter concern for general education is emerging as a reaction both against narrow career specialization and the diluted approach that has been taken to general education during the past twenty years.

Limited resources may result in more new programs using present courses from different disciplines in new combinations. Interdisciplinary courses provide coverage in such new fields as environmental studies, urban affairs, and mass communications (Stewart and Harvey, 1975). Rather than organizing new departments, new major programs can be established by bringing together faculty and courses from existing departments.

Graduate programs are being affected by the forces of change.

Doctoral programs have been hit by a decline in demand for people with doctorates and in federal funds supporting doctoral students and research. Master's programs may be affected in different ways. Continuing advanced educational needs may result in more people pursuing master's degrees as a terminal degree, especially in professional fields.

The continuing rapid changes in knowledge and technology, the increasing competition for good jobs and promotions, and the influx of nontraditional students all indicate a much greater emphasis on continuing adult education. More states are requiring that licensed professionals periodically take additional courses. Continuing general education for adults is another emerging opportunity. More adults, who have emphasized professional work in their educational program, seek an occasional course from the arts and sciences to enrich their lives (Millett, 1977).

Some institutions are providing a much greater variety of time formats for courses — classes that meet early mornings, evenings, and weekends; courses lasting only three to six weeks; and other variations. Courses are also being offered in a greater number of off-campus locations. Adapting times and places may be more important in addressing the needs of nontraditional students than new programs and courses.

The new era of limited resources has resulted in greater concerns for accountability in higher education. Universities will have to devise new or better ways of evaluating programs in terms of viability and cost, strengths and weaknesses, and student achievement. Traditionally, program evaluation has been little more than the ongoing assessment of courses to determine which ones to change, add and drop (Glenny and others, 1976). Evaluations of programs will identify improvements needed and serve as a guide to directing scarce resources, and in extreme cases, to determining whether to consolidate or discontinue programs.

Student Programs. The change in the mix of students who attend college, along with the decline in enrollments, will have significant repercussions on the kinds of student programs needed. Nontraditional students (older students, married students, and working students) need different kinds of student services and activities than traditional students. Student services will need to address new student needs and problems and thus contribute toward adaptive survival of the university and its programs (Stewart and Harvey, 1975).

In order to plan adequately for faculty recruitment, program changes, and budgets, colleges and universities must adopt new approaches to recruitment and enrollment projections. Traditional enrollment projection techniques, based on extrapolated trends of eighteen to twenty-one-year-olds, do not predict accurately in the new era. It is therefore necessary to identify the basic underlying factors that affect enrollments, for example, job markets, financial aid, and attitudes toward college (Seeley and others, 1974). Recruiting must also become more sophisticated. It must be based on information generated by research studies concerning potential student markets and strategies for reaching each group.

Admission procedures, registration, and financial aid policies all need to be adapted to the new kinds of students. Setting admission deadlines one month before classes begin, requiring official transcripts for work at several universities over the past twenty years, requiring test scores for middle-aged professionals, and then having long delays in processing all have negative effects on most nontraditional students. Financial aid must be available to part-time students, women, and older students, including senior citizens. Finally registration must be held during a range of times and places—not simply on campus during regular office hours.

The new students have different needs for advising, counseling, and career planning and placement (Johansen and McNulty, 1977). Most older students will not need guidance in choosing a major or assistance in finding an entry-level job, but they will need help in career and life planning, in adjusting to college (taking tests, studying, and so on) and in changing jobs.

Declining enrollments will increase concerns for retaining present students. The academic skills of entering students, some of whom had marginal high school preparation and others who have not been in a classroom in years, can be remediated through special programs. Beyond assisting those with academic difficulties, attention should be given to sustaining the enrollment of students in good standing. As students increasingly take an "in-and-out" approach to education, ways of sequencing classes, facilitating readmission, and finding channels to communicate with this group pose new problems.

On-campus life and extracurricular activities must also adapt to the new nontraditional students. They have many more interests competing for their time—careers, families, and outside activities—and their interests are different. While dances, pep rallies, and student government may not attract them, they are interested in exhibits, concerts, outstanding speakers, and career-oriented activities.

Faculty. The faculty will feel the greatest impact from limited growth. As enrollments decline and resources level off, faculty positions will be threatened. The number of faculty positions, which grew from 248,000 in 1965 to 412,000 ten years later, is projected to increase until 1982, and then decline an estimated 30,000 positions by 1990 (Cartter, 1975).

The effects on faculty will be great. Faculty members in some fields will be faced with the problems of survival, and will find fewer opportunities to move to other institutions. Changing and conflicting demands are being placed upon faculty — to maintain student enroll-ments, to teach new courses, to serve nontraditional students at differ-ent times and locations, to maintain research and community service under more rigorous standards, and to participate in institutional gov-ernance. Salaries, relative to inflation and other professionals, have leveled off. Individual faculty members thus find themselves in com-petitive situations and face more personal stress.

Institutions also face difficult situations in regard to faculty. They are concerned about being able to retain vitality by hiring new people and with having flexibility to respond to emerging fields of study. A few universities have modeled how the faculty will look in the future, using different assumptions about student-faculty ratios, tenure rates, time in rank, mobility, and retirements (Bowker, 1974; Cartter, 1975). These models provide a way to anticipate potential problems and permit planned actions before a crisis is imminent.

The rate at which new faculty are tenured has been found crucial. There is a trend toward faculties' becoming heavily tenured (the percent holding tenure climbed from 53 percent in 1968 to 69 percent only four years later) and becoming much older (42 percent were over age forty-five in 1972, which could increase to 63 percent in 1990) (Cartter, 1975). Lack of new faculty positions is compounded by the fact that only 4 percent of experienced faculty leave higher education each year, and that the retirement and death rate is less than 2 percent each year.

Tenure review processes, which became more rigorous in the 1970s, are likely to become more stringent until an average of only 50 percent of those eligible for consideration for tenure will actually be ten-ured. The percent tenured can also be reduced by identifying a set number of nontenure appointments, including limited term, visiting, and part-time appointments. Part-time appointments are likely to increase because of the institutional flexibility they provide, because they provide coverage in some specialties, and because the salaries for them are lower. Increasing part-time appointments will require clarify-ing their status and formulating policies on recruitment, supervision, salaries, benefits, and evaluation for part-time faculty.

Concerns in the 1980s for protecting positions, maintaining salaries, the depressed job market, the shifting of power to state bureaucracies, and working conditions may lead to more faculties' turning to collective bargaining (Didham and others, 1976). In 1974, 13 percent of all faculty were covered by collective bargaining agreements; since then, growth has continued at a moderate rate (Glenny and others, 1976).

The forces of change will place a much greater emphasis on faculty development and evaluation. As faculty members stay in the same positions and at the same institutions longer, they will need to remain current in their subject areas and add new skills, such as working with computers. Faculty development needs will escalate, however, to include developing new allied fields and different ways of teaching, advising, and working with nontraditional students. Some faculty may even undertake complete retraining for second careers in higher education.

Much greater emphasis will be placed on faculty evaluation because of the tough decisions that will have to be made on tenure, promotions, salary increases, and reductions in staff. Over three fourths of the universities and colleges report systematic efforts to evaluate faculty during the 1970s (Glenny and others, 1976). In addition to generally more rigorous evaluations, the base of inputs is broadening to include student, peer, and self-evaluations as well as evaluations by administrators. Strains are emerging concerning which factors should enter into evaluations. Issues of across-the-board leveling versus greater differentiation on the basis of merit are also being debated (Lee and Bowen, 1975).

Governance and Administration. The processes of governance and administration within universities will be affected by the forces of change. Planning, budgeting, the flow of information, and the roles of faculty and administrators will feel the effects. The most obvious problem area will be resource development and management.

Relatively stable resources with declining purchasing power will necessitate far more extensive internal reallocation of resources. New programs, which are needed not only to remain vital but to keep enrollments from declining even more, will require allocation. Reallocation will also be necessary to maintain levels of quality in some programs and to reflect internal shifts in enrollments among existing programs. In the new era, budgeting will be more visible, more sophisticated, more closely tied to academic planning, will take a longer-run point of view, involve more participants, and be more subject to rigidities and higher-level controls (Lee and Bowen, 1975).

Resource constraints will place even greater emphasis on expanding the resource base. Beyond trying to increase enrollments, public universities will search for more effective ways to present their needs to state legislatures. Higher education, which found tying budgets to enrollments advantageous during the great growth years, now needs to find ways to uncouple the two. A greater number of universities will also learn how to tap the federal government more effectively. Greater governmental support, however, requires a better understanding of how government works and more attention and resources devoted to the effort by the universities (Stewart and Harvey, 1975). Private giving will also receive greater emphasis, especially as public institutions borrow a chapter from private universities.

To better anticipate problems and make intelligent responses, universities will increasingly emphasize planning and information systems. A wide range of information is needed about the present and the future to provide data-based decisions and realism (Cartter, 1975). Planning will be extended from physical planning to long-range planning by departments. Of necessity, planning must be based on an understanding and assessment of present programs.

Administrative processes, and the people who administer them, will feel the forces of change. The skills and qualities desired in administrators will change. Administrators, like faculty members, will need development programs to gain the skills needed in the new age. Likewise, administrators, as well as faculty, will be systematically evaluated.

Consistent with the collegial approach to governance, faculty members will need to be involved in the new kinds of difficult decisions facing universities. Some procedures for providing meaningful influence on decisions, such as committee structures, will need to be developed. The willingness of faculties to devote significant time and emotional energy to inherently difficult problems and unpopular decisions will need reinforcement. The new era poses potential threats to collegiality. Therefore, a sense of community, interdependence, and joint venture will need to be engendered.

The resolution of the problems of the 1980s will necessitate effective communication. Internal communications processes did not keep pace as universities grew and became more complex. Now the difficult decisions and tensions of the new era place even greater importance on the flow of information. External communications will need to convey different messages to different groups, such as potential nontraditional students. In turn, the flow of information from students, alumni, and the public to the university will need to be actively encouraged.

Differences in Impacts. There are many crosscurrents beneath the surface of steady state conditions. Not all colleges and universities are going to be affected the same by the forces of change. Neither the forces themselves nor the implications and effects are the same from one place to another, from one kind of institution to another, or from one area to another within the same university. Therefore, while there are general national trends in higher education, each university must analyze its own situation, the forces of change in motion within its own environment, and the special implications of the changes.

Differences in the forces of change in geographic areas are clearly illustrated by the differences in enrollment projections and budget increases by states. Some states will have increases ranging from less than 1 percent to 20 percent in the number of eighteen-year-olds, while others will experience a decline in the number of this group ranging from 10 to 43 percent (Henderson, 1977). State funds for higher education have also changed unevenly. From 1969 to 1979, 17 states increased over 250 percent (primarily southern and western states) and, at the other extreme, nine states increased their contributions to higher education less than 150 percent in ten years (*Chronicle,* October 9, 1979).

Situations vary from one kind of institution to another. Larger institutions may be able to absorb more of the impacts. Other areas within the university can temporarily offset or buffer changes, and the larger university may have better access to some resources (Lee and Bowen, 1975). The great dependence of private colleges on tuition causes them to be disproportionately affected by changes in enrollments. Additional examples of the differential impact of change are that community colleges may continue to grow, urban universities may have an advantage of having more nontraditional students, regional comprehensive universities may have overexpanded, and major doctoral-research universities may have suffered with declines in research funds and demand for doctorates.

The impacts are very uneven within universities. Zero growth in enrollments may mask significant internal shifts. Some of the changes are more basic and predictable, while others are harder to understand and even harder to predict. Despite the difficulties, internal shifts, which are compounded by each institution's own unique history and situation, must be addressed.

The history of higher education is unlikely to relegate the past ten years or the next ten years to obscurity. The expansionist dreams of the 1960s have been left behind, and the harsh realities of the 1980s lie ahead. The forces of change are in motion. They create an uncertain future, posing problems and offering opportunities. Universities can anticipate the changes and develop strategies for responding creatively. To do so provides the basis for shaping the kind of university they will be and for facing the future with confidence.

References

Bowker, A. "Managing the Faculty Resources in the Steady State." Paper presented at the American Council on Education meeting, San Diego, California, October 10, 1974.

Cartter, A. M. (Ed.). *New Directions for Institutional Research: Assuring Academic Progress Without Growth*, no. 6. San Francisco: Jossey-Bass, 1975.

Chronicle of Higher Education, September 24, 1979, p. 9; October 9, 1979, p. 9, p. 13.

Didham, J. R., and others. *Limited Growth in Higher Education*. Ann Arbor: University of Michigan Center for the Study of Higher Education, 1976.

Glenny, L. A. and others. *Presidents Confront Reality: From Edifice Complex to University Without Walls*. San Francisco: Jossey-Bass, 1976.

Henderson, C. *Changes in Enrollment by 1985*. Washington, D.C.: American Council on Education, 1977.

Johansen, R., and McNulty, M. *Alternative Futures and Postsecondary Education in Pennsylvania*. Menlo Park, Calif.: Institute for the Future, 1977.

Johansen, R. and Samuel, P. A. *Future Societal Developments and Postsecondary Education*. Menlo Park, Calif.: Institute for the Future, 1977.

Kreps, J. "Higher Education in a Low-Growth, High-Inflation Economy." Paper presented at the American Council on Education Annual Meeting, San Diego, California, October 10, 1974.

Lee, E. C. and Bowen, F. M. *Managing Multicampus Systems: Effective Administration in an Unsteady State*. San Francisco: Jossey-Bass, 1975.

Millett, J. D. *Managing Change in Higher Education*. Washington, D.C.: Academy for Educational Development, 1977.

Morrison, P. *The Demographic Context of Educational Policy Planning*. Santa Monica, Calif.: Rand Corporation, 1976.

Seeley, J. and others. *Projecting College and University Enrollments*. Ann Arbor: University of Michigan Center for the Study of Higher Education, 1974.

Stewart, C., and Harvey, T. (Eds.). *New Directions for Higher Education: Strategies for Significant Survival*, no. 12. San Francisco: Jossey-Bass, 1975.

Donald D. Christenson was assistant vice president for Academic Affairs and project director for the W. K. Kellogg Leadership and Management Development project at Wichita State University and is currently professor in the College of Business Administration at Wichita State.

*The situation today demands that change be approached in a
positive way, or institutions of higher education run the risk
of becoming victims rather than effective managers of change.*

Planned Change in Institutions
of Higher Learning

Philip C. Winstead

Change is the process of altering, modifying, or transforming; it may
entail termination, growth, substitution, replacement, or simply passing from one phase to another. Planned change is a deliberate process
designed to solve a problem or improve a condition. The concept of
planned change in higher education is built on five underlying propositions (Bennis and others, 1961; Gardner, 1964):

1. There is a need to create planning mechanisms for renewal
   and redirection to counteract the built-in bias of complex
   institutions to maintain the status quo.
2. There is a need for leadership within an institution to initiate
   and encourage these mechanisms.
3. Renewal mechanisms should be based on valid knowledge
   and objective research.
4. Renewal mechanisms should include an internal planning
   specialist to facilitate the change process.
5. There should be a consciousness of the desired direction and
   extent of movement in the whole system rather than isolated
   interventions.

G. Hipps (Ed.). *New Directions for Institutional Research: Effective Planned Change Strategies*, no. 33.
San Francisco: Jossey-Bass, March 1982.

Planned change in this context deals with developing new and better processes and relationships in response to changing needs and expectations. In order for it to be successful, it must usually be fostered by the top campus leadership. The people already in charge normally serve as the key causal agents, since the status quo is being altered. Effective planned change cannot, in most cases, be brought about solely by outsiders.

In addition, a successful planned change process requires intelligent, responsible participation by all members of the college or university community in gathering data, analyzing capabilities, setting goals and objectives, developing and executing programs of action, allocating resources, and evaluating results.

Need for Planned Change

There are a number of educational situations that substantiate the need for planned change. Some of the problems that create the need are internal, and some are environmental. Although there is a close interdependence of these two kinds of problems, change efforts tend to focus on one type or the other. Because of the interdependence, however, changes in either internal or external relationships will be accompanied by changes in the other area.

One of the internal problems that can point up a need for planned change in a college or university is the distribution of power. Power highly concentrated in the hands of a few can foster resentment by the majority of the institution's constituents. On the other hand, the power may be so diffused that decision making is cumbersome and laborious. Both examples are indicative of defective power structures that call for a new and more appropriate organization of power for decision making. Planned change can create a broader, participative base for the power structure so that decisions will more accurately reflect the needs of all the constituents.

A second internal problem is lack of adequate communication among the constituents of an institution. A breakdown in communication in any area can cause difficulty in the functioning of the entire organization. A communication network should provide links among the constituents; in a university these constituents would include administrators, faculty, students, board of trustees, advisory councils, and community. In the hierarchical structure that is characteristic of most colleges and universities, communication is necessary between the different levels of the structure to share perceptions of the needs of the institution and to convey information to the persons involved about what they could do to meet the needs. Planned change can improve poor communication.

Planned change can address external situations that involve the relationship between the institution and its environment. Sometimes there is a discrepancy between the environment as it actually exists and as it is perceived by the institution's constituents. When either the institution or those in its environment sift their perceptions through a bias instead of objective standards of interpretation, or when either interprets messages from the other using a frame of reference that differs significantly from the frame of reference of the other, the relationship between them suffers. Planned change can establish a common frame of reference for more accurate perception.

Another external factor influencing the need for planned change is the financial climate in which higher education must operate. Planned change can help colleges and universities set priorities among their goals and make appropriate resource allocation decisions in order to try to offset the negative effects of inflation, steady state enrollment, and lessening of public confidence in higher education.

Resistance to Change

Despite this evidence for the need for change, there is often ambivalence about change. While people sometimes want change, they fear its consequences. Within an institution there may be conflicting pressures for both change and the status quo. Those who want to keep things as they are are satisfied and fear change will disrupt their relationships, reduce their power, and certainly will create more work for them. Some of the forces that may work against change are the faculty members' loyalties within disciplines, rigidity of the faculty tenure system, weak leadership structure, and longstanding tradition. Furthermore, college and university administrators who try to plan dynamically from a changing base are overwhelmed by the volume of data impinging upon them by the need to coordinate the processes of an organization that serves numerous constituents.

Strategies for Planned Change

Planned change in an educational institution should be based on a program that includes (1) receiving information from the constituencies served by the institution, (2) devising means whereby that information can be processed so that agreement on what the information means can be reached and revised by the constituencies, (3) formulating plans and programs to achieve the organizational goals and objectives, (4) implementing appropriate actions to accomplish the goals and objectives, and (5) evaluating those actions. Organizational development procedures, information systems, and institutional research techniques should support formal management in bringing about change (see Figure 1). Since the informational input is constantly changing, a dynamic process is required that will facilitate clarifying and revising goals, objectives, and strategies and will be adaptable to meet the changing needs of the constituencies as they arise. A planned change specialist is of utmost importance. This person is not one who dictates change, but one who oversees the change process and serves as an internal change agent for the institution.

Figure 1. Change Process

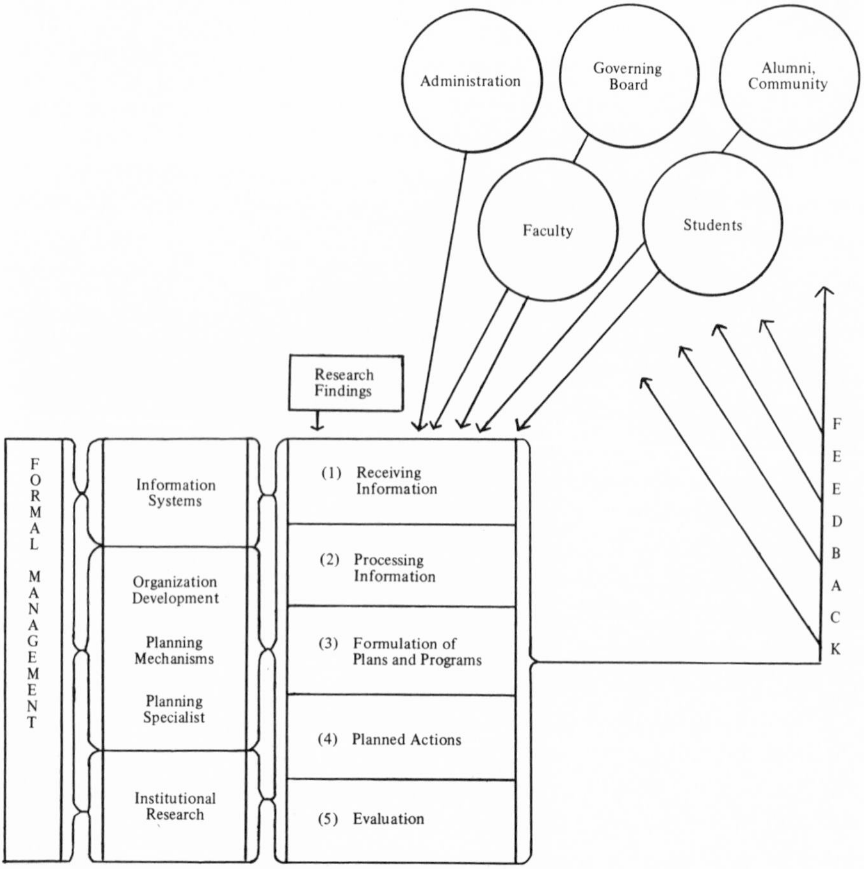

Because planned change deals with developing new processes and relationships, there is a variety of strategies for effecting change. Havelock was one of the first to provide a general change model in which he combined three popular strategies (problem solving; social interaction; and research, development, and diffusion) that have come to be called his linkage theory (Havelock, 1973). He believed that planned change could be accomplished when the person or group saw a need for change, a solution to the problem, and possible application of the solution.

More recently, Lindquist has described four change strategies: rational planning, social interaction, human problem solving, and political (Lindquist, 1978). Rational planning rests on a rational sequence of planning activities that, when developed and tested, should be accepted because they are based on valid evidence and sound reason. Rational planning strategies use institutional research and planning offices and are based on the premise that with reliable information, decision making will be more reasonable. Social interaction strategies bring about awareness, trial, and eventual adoption of change by using people in already existing social networks to introduce innovations. Human problem solving strategies use skilled intervention in human relations to diagnose and remove psychological barriers or problems that are obstacles to people's willingness to change. Building powerful coalitions among interests and obtaining authoritative decisions to ensure that people change their attitudes and behaviors are the principal political strategies.

While it is convenient to categorize change into a neat typology, the more common practice is interaction of the prevailing types. At times, the appropriate mode is social interaction. Consensus is obtained through the discussions of colleagues who are in a position to effect change. For example, two deans may agree on the need for an interdisciplinary course that combines areas in each of their schools and may implement the process of course design, course approval, and course scheduling. At other times, the appropriate change strategy is human problem solving. In this case, one dean, seeing the necessity for cooperation with another dean, may call for third-party intervention to arbitrate the problem that is hindering the joint effort. Still again, the change strategy may be political. One dean goes directly to his superior and obtains a mandate based upon the realities of the given situation. Finally, the change strategy may be rational planning. Here the dean reasons out his proposal, gathers supporting evidence, and makes a detailed presentation to those who will be affected by the change. In a sense of participative cooperation, those in positions of responsibility decide on a course of action consistent with the goals and objectives of the institution and the environmental factors impinging upon the decision.

While each of the separate strategies or change models is important and occurs frequently in various situations, planned change must start with a rational approach to develop the most effective formal mode. An institution need not scrap tradition and start over. Neither should an institution fail to recognize that different situations call for different strategies. The key is to recognize the critical ingredients of each situation and use the appropriate change strategies, but maintain rational planning as the underlying concept. In fact, it is suggested that institutions move toward a rational planning model through a gradual process of expanding participation in planning, behavior modification sessions, and formal planning activities. To be sure, resistance to planned change in higher education will continue. The complexity of colleges and universities and the diffusion of the decision-making process will be among the most frequently cited reasons that "it won't work." Yet many organizations, both business and educational, have demonstrated that change can be planned.

A Suggested Planned Change Model

Many educators are beginning to recognize that no phase of institutional development can be left to chance, impulse, or coercion. There is, moreover, the belief, held by many, that scientific knowledge in organization theory is now sufficiently developed that it can contribute greatly to improving college and university organization and administration.

Against this background, one model to assist colleges and universities in introducing a continuous process of institutional development that facilitates normal administrative operations and, at the same time, encourages and supports constructive orderly change is a decentralized, participative one that emphasizes systematic planning and management by objectives. The proposed model rests on three basic premises. The first is that the educational processes, organizational structures, and administrative operations of colleges and universities are so complex that it is difficult for these institutions to be effectively responsive to the needs for change without adequate procedures for comprehensive planning and decision making. These procedures must be based on the setting of institutional goals and objectives, methods for properly allocating human and financial resources, management by objectives, and continuous evaluation. Such a systems approach to organizing, planning, decision making, and evaluating can demonstrate that a college or university can achieve a higher degree of educational effectiveness than it has been able to achieve in the past.

The second premise is that improved research techniques for collecting and analyzing information exist on most campuses, and analytical tools are available that can support improved planning techniques.

The third premise is that the complexities of the change process and the comprehensiveness of the model require on-campus, professional support to coordinate and expedite this approach to college and university administration. Not only must there be a formal office of institutional planning, but it must be properly staffed and supported.

The model suggested has three components: organizational development, information systems, and institutional research. The first of these components is a process of participatory decision making and institutional self-renewal that integrates the needs and goals of individuals in the institution with the goals and objectives of the institution. It involves procedures for clarifying goals, deriving measurable objectives from goals, implementing a comprehensive approach to management by objectives, securing a planned change specialist, and systematic planning. In the model, management by objectives is based upon the premise that no individual can direct all of the activities of a complex organization; but if the emphasis can be shifted to outcomes, even the most complex structure can be managed. The purpose of planning is to optimize performance, regardless of what may happen in the environment.

The second component of the model is information systems. This component is a support service and provides the means for gathering, compiling, storing, retrieving, analyzing, and reporting data for institutional planning and decision making. However, establishing information systems suited to the institution's needs requires more than access to a computer. Cost-effective information systems must provide the data required for day-to-day decision making as well as for long-range planning.

Information systems most useful are generalized data-management systems, which can be either manual or computer based. The data systems chosen should be flexible with respect to content and reporting requirements. They should be efficient with respect to time and cost required to initiate them, and later, to modify them as new information requirements are defined and new data elements are identified. The result should be to provide the decision maker with current and comprehensive information in focus at the times and places where the decisions and plans are being made.

The institutional research component is another support service and can provide the research designs, measurement methods, statistical techniques, and other tools of systematic inquiry needed to make research-based decisions. It provides both the "why" and the "how" for gathering and analyzing relevant data, formulating alternatives for sound decision making, and monitoring progress toward the attainment of institutional goals and objectives. Institutional research can be the means by which a college or university searches for the truth about itself; what it is accomplishing and how well; what key constituents think it should be accomplishing and why; what its resources are and how effectively they are being used; what potential resources are not being tapped; and what changes should be made in policies, procedures, and programs, and methods for making those changes are feasible.

Planned Change Specialist

Success of the planning process in the model rests heavily on the planned change specialist. This is a senior-level, highly professional role.

Functions and Activities. The characteristics, functions, and activities of the planned change specialist are likely to include the following:

- An internal catalyst for change
- A link to national technologies, innovations, and research and development systems
- A resource to those engaged in institutional planning and decision making
- Continuous research to improve institutional planning and decision making
- A sensitivity to the changing demands in higher education
- Familiarity with the professional literature and data sources for monitoring innovative developments in higher education
- The identification of promising alternatives to current practices
- A resource to those responsible for clarifying institutional goals
- The monitoring of progress toward institutional goals

- Assisting in deriving measurable objectives for the institution
- Mediator in various conflict situations
- A "question asker" and an "idea stimulator"
- Assistance in maintaining an effective internal communications network
- Coordination of the institutional research efforts
- The encouragement of knowledge utilization in the decision making process
- A resource to various task groups and other ad hoc committees
- A disseminator of internal innovations
- A creator of appropriate institutional renewal processes

Necessary Knowledge and Skills. To accomplish these tasks, the planned change specialist must possess certain knowledge and skills and must have adequate resources available to him. He should be responsible for, or have full access to, the office of institutional research or comparable research assistance as well as to data processing services. He should develop some expertise in organization development, management science techniques, evaluation, and in facilitating the processes of communication among people. He should also be wise in the judicious introduction of new types of data into the operations of the institution.

He should be familiar with the major issues confronting higher education in general and his institution in particular. He should be familiar with the process of developmental planning and decision making. He should have the skills and resources required to draw upon relevant information from the literature and the latest research and experimentation done elsewhere. Finally, he should have a thorough knowledge of an accepted long-range planning process for colleges and universities.

A Planning Process

A systematic planning process is one of the key elements of planned change. Planning, however, can be just as complex or just as simple as one wants it to be. The planning process that follows is not intended to produce a plan as much as it is a "thinking process" that allows for thorough and systematic examination of alternatives. (For a more complete description of the suggested planning process, see Green and Winstead, 1975.) It brings into focus the kind of information that is needed to make decisions, yet it is flexible and adaptable to a constantly changing environment. In the past, many people have believed that the primary purpose of planning is to produce a plan, and the process of planning was designed accordingly. As a result, many plans have not been useful for long because there was no process for their revision or for adapting them to changing conditions. Recently, more and more college administrators are coming to realize that a plan may be a valuable benefit of planning but not the primary purpose. The real purpose of planning is to get the best results regardless of what happens in the future. Having a plan per se can even be detrimental if the plan cannot be changed easily in the event of unforeseen developments.

In the model, systematic planning includes the following steps or activities:

- Identification and evaluation of problems and opportunities
- Clarification and evaluation of problems and opportunities
- Determination of priorities
- Analysis and evaluation of capabilities
- Development and execution of program of action
- Identification and monitoring of future developments that will have a major impact on performance or results
- Allocation of essential resources
- Acceptance and support of key people who are involved or affected

These steps or activities, which are continuous and interactive, can only be accomplished through planning. They need not occur exactly in this order, and sometimes certain of them will occur concurrently.

While all aspects of the planning process are important, four stand out. The first is the needs assessment component of the process. Needs assessment can take the shape of a SWOTs analysis. SWOTs is an acronym for a self-appraisal in which each organizational unit examines the Strengths, Weaknesses, Opportunities, and Threats within that unit. Next, the departmental SWOTs can be consolidated into a university-wide analysis. As a part of the process, needs can be weighed against the needs of the individual unit as well as the university as a whole. As a result, objectives can be formulated that maximize strengths, minimize weaknesses, capitalize on opportunities, or eliminate threats.

The second important aspect is establishing goals and deriving measurable objectives from these goals. A goal is defined as a statement of general intent that provides focus and direction but is not necessarily measurable. An objective is an estimate of a very important future result that one believes can and should be accomplished through his or her own efforts, that the institution is willing and able to pay for, and which is measurable. The planning model is based on systems theory, and the use of goals and objectives related to the SWOTs analysis or needs assessment ensures that goals and objectives are related directly to the most important needs of the individual unit and the institution.

The third important aspect of the planning process is the development and execution of programs of action. An objective is a delusion unless there are clearly defined and budgeted "programs of action" designed to accomplish the agreed upon objective. In the planning model it is recommended that a standard procedure be used that includes outlining the nature and scope of the implementation plan, the objective or objectives pursued, who is responsible, the schedule of the tasks, and the resources needed to support the program or project. The appropriate programs of action ensure the linkage between needs assessment and approved objectives.

The fourth important aspect of systematic planning is evaluation. Evaluative procedures should be included that will provide formative and summative data on the planning process, the plan itself, and the outcomes or results of the activities undertaken. These evaluation steps complete the formal planning cycle and ensure integration of planning activities with the needs, goals, and objectives of the institution.

Implementation of the Model

It has been suggested that the implementation of a rational planned change model be gradual. It should be gradual, but it should also be consistent and deliberate. There should be appropriate policies to guide the decentralized, participatory process. For example, an institutional governance policy designed to support a rational planning model would include language such as:

> Those responsible for the governance of this university are committed to a concept of decentralized, participative management based on appropriate delegation, without abdication, or responsibility and authority. The responsibility for planning and control shall be placed as close as practical to the point of execution. Every person in charge of a department, program, or activity should formulate plans and recommendations for his own area of responsibility that can be coordinated with other activities and can be consolidated at higher levels to support the goals, objectives, and policies of the university.

This definition of decentralized participation, however, should not be interpreted to infringe upon the authority and responsibility of those serving in official line capacities within the organization.

Consensus is extremely important in a rational planning model but should not be seen as necessarily democratic. Reason should prevail, and propositions should be supported by valid evidence. All of those affected by a decision should be allowed to have appropriate input, but final decisions, whether or not the result of consensus, should rest in the hands of those charged with responsibility for making such decisions. This stance should not detract, however, from the desirability of using the rational planning process to improve communication and to upgrade the quality of information upon which plans and decisions are made, thereby creating a situation in which consensus of goals, objectives, and priorities is more likely. An important consideration when making a decision in the absence of consensus is for the decision maker to make a conscious effort to weigh all the evidence carefully before making the decision.

The most feasible implementation strategy for the rational planned change model is to create the needed planning mechanisms (for example, the formal model, the planning specialist, and the visible commitment of the top leadership), establish appropriate policies and procedures to support the model, gain the acceptance and support of those with program responsibility through open discussions in order to minimize surprise, and create a management information system that will supply the basic data needs of the model. Most important, however, is to adhere to the maxim, "progressive accomplishment rather than postponed perfection."

Change is the altering of tradition and the modifying of patterned ways. The trading of a known and secure environment for uncertainty and the unknown is an inevitable consequence of change. Furthermore, there is ambiguity about change. There is recognition that change can be an improvement, but there is also recognition that change can produce trauma and loss of security.

Planned change is a deliberate process designed to solve a problem or improve a condition. It is based on objective research, formal interventions, and the use of systematic planning procedures. It is designed to alleviate fear and uncertainty and to foster excitement, institutional renewal, and personal and organizational growth. While resistance to change is a reality, appropriate planned change strategies can overcome inertia and built-in biases toward the status quo. To ensure the success of the planned change process, it is necessary to employ a planned change specialist and a formal, systematic planning process.

The role of planned change specialist, in addition to using organization development and behavioral science techniques, should include appropriate use of a process of planning that is responsive to changing conditions, provides a better method of developing appropriate programs of action, minimizes the degree to which one is taken by surprise, optimizes performance in a changing environment, and, most important, causes good things to happen. Good planning and planned change get good results.

Systematic planning as a way to change does not solve all the problems or answer all the questions of an institution. It can provide focus and direction, cause priorities of the institution to be decided upon, see that alternatives are considered, and clearly identify those who are responsible for accomplishing certain results. The situation today demands that change be approached in a positive way, or institutions of higher education run the real risk of becoming the victims of change rather than effective managers of change.

References

Bennis, W. G., Benne, K. D., and Chin, R. (Eds.). *The Planning of Change: Readings in the Applied Behavioral Sciences.* New York: Holt, Rinehart and Winston, 1961.

Gardner, J. W. *Self-Renewal: The Individual and the Innovative Society.* New York: Harper & Row, 1964.

Green, E. J., and Winstead, P. C. "Systematic Institutional Planning." *Educational Technology,* 1975, *15* (7), 33–35.

Havelock, R. G. *The Change Agent's Guide to Innovation in Education.* Englewood Cliffs, N.J.: Educational Technology Publications, 1973.

Lindquist, J. *Strategies for Change.* Berkeley, Calif.: Pacific Soundings Press, 1978.

Philip C. Winstead is coordinator of Institutional Planning and Research and professor of education at Furman University. He was codirector of the W. K. Kellogg-sponsored project, Faculty Development in Academic Planning: An Approach to Institutional Renewal, and is presently director of Programs for Faculty Development at Furman.

Both targets of the change effort—people and structures—
should be approached in tandem and functionally integrated.

Team Leadership Development

Velma Pomrenke

In the past decades, several conceptualizations of change strategies have emerged. Based on Kurt Lewin's "freezing, unfreezing, refreezing" model, Lippitt, Watson, and Westley (1958) suggest a phase theory of planned change. A change agent must raise awareness of the need for change; establish the relationship between the organization and the change agent; move toward change through diagnosis, examination of alternatives, and choice of an implementation plan; stabilize the change; and terminate the change agent's relationship to the organization.

Another approach to change conceptualizes four classes of interacting variables as components of an interdependent system (Leavitt, 1965). The variables are task, technology, people, and structure. Change strategies can be applied to one or another of these classes of variables toward the goal of accomplishing the task, the primary output variable.

Chin and Benne (1969) present a three-part model for effecting change: empirical-rational, normative-reeducative, and power-coercive strategies. The empirical-rational strategy is based on the assumption that people will use reason and rationality to identify and implement needed changes. The normative-reeducative strategy

G. Hipps (Ed.). *New Directions for Institutional Research: Effective Planned Change Strategies*, no. 33.
San Francisco: Jossey-Bass, March 1982.

assumes that human needs are satisfied by interacting with others and the environment. Therefore, according to this part of the model, change is best achieved by altering norms, roles, and relationships within an organization. The power-coercive strategy assumes that changes are best implemented through agents who possess political, economic, moral or personal power.

Change can be managed in different ways. On the one hand, organizational change can be mandated by those who have the power and access to resources to implement their commands. Conversely, change can be implemented through processes that recognize the impact of change on people and through leadership principles that ensure a higher probability of acceptance of change.

Many times, enforcing change seems the only way in which resistance can be overcome, and new procedures introduced. It appears to bring immediate results. Students of change theory, however, are in fairly close agreement that in the long run, mandated change is counterproductive. Tensions are increased, defensiveness is raised, and constant policing is frequently necessary to monitor enforced change.

Change is facilitated, however, when it is communicated fully to everyone involved; when those who are affected by change are involved in the decision making; when fears are countered with factual information; when it is made as acceptable as possible; when it is placed on a trial basis; when it has the commitment of top management; when structure is altered to support the change; and when specific actions are developed in organizations that will make operational the elements just enumerated (Deep, 1978).

Universities are composed of many subgroups that share a common purpose — educating a human being — as they function in separate but interrelated ways. To accomplish change in universities, it is important to be aware of where, among the subsystems, change can most readily be implemented. In addition, because universities are complex systems, change in one subsystem will inevitably affect another subsystem. The astute change agent will in fact pay careful attention to where change is introduced so that there is a high likelihood of its taking root and branching out to permeate the total organization.

Organizational change is most often successful when there is commitment to and support for change by top management. Still, as Kahn (1977) suggests, how and when top management will be involved in the change effort is a critical variable. He writes: "Does it mean that the top of the organization must change before any part can do so? Does it mean that the people at the top of the organization must actively support the proposed program of change without necessarily becoming 'trainees' themselves? Or does it mean merely that some degree of top echelon sanction for a new enterprise of organizational development must be visible in order for others to accept the proposed changes?" (p. 224).

The issue of power—personal or positional—must be faced if change is to be accomplished in the university (Baldridge, 1971). Although the style of decision making in a university may appear to be highly consensual and collegial, the truth may be that the dynamics of consensus building are highly flavored with the taste for power. To ignore conflict, defensive positions, and the potential for rough-and-tumble politics in universities, is to ignore dynamics that profoundly affect the management of change. The crucial task, it appears, is to build relationships in which conflict can be resolved in a positive manner, in which the need for power positions (competition) is decreased, and in which the effectiveness of power redistribution (collaboration) is increased.

Dynamic external environments; enforced versus facilitated change; systems dynamics of the university; varying difficulty of achieving change at the levels of knowledge, attitudes, behavior, and group or organization; commitment and support from top management; the role of power; and the variety of conceptualizations about change strategies are all important considerations when planning change and suggest that good change strategies must be multivariate and take into account the interrelationships among the variables. When one is dealing with multivariate situations, models can provide a way in which underlying principles can be identified and thus present a semblance of order and coherence. Two general models for bringing about change are the structural model and the people model.

Structural Model

The structural approach to organizational change focuses on what an individual in an organization is *expected* to do rather than what he or she does. Therefore, it gives primary attention to such variables as admission criteria, number of graduates, communication patterns, faculty policies, decision-making structures, grievance procedures, position descriptions, membership rules, and so on. The assumption is that changes in these structural variables will cause human beings to act more effectively and efficiently.

The structural approach to change is rooted in the scientific management and administrative science movements. The major theme of these organizational design theories is that there is one best way to *organize* work (time and motion studies); and when that "best way" is implemented, productivity will increase. It is easy and tempting to apply the same principle to organizational change, that is, to assume that individuals can be changed or "molded" by the organizational structure; change the structure, therefore, change the person.

In the same vein, Katz and Kahn (1978) describe the organization as a system of roles. Role behaviors are defined as those behaviors that are expected of individuals and will result in a predictable outcome. Thus, the expectation that a faculty member will appear in the classroom leads to the expectation that an educated student will be produced. When the expected behavior descriptions are changed, it is assumed that the behavior of the individual will change. To pursue the analogy, if a faculty member was expected to appear in a classroom in informal dress and sit with the students instead of standing in front of them, interactions with students would perhaps increase, and, some would say, the real education process would be set in motion. Although this approach appears to take people into account, the variable being treated is expectations, and expectations are related primarily to the structural characteristics of an organization. One might believe, however, that the expectations or role descriptions are modified by each role incumbent. The key word, however, is *modified.* To modify is indeed to change, but only in very minor ways, which may have little impact on the group or organizational level. A strong case, therefore, can be made that behavior and attitude change can best be brought about by changing structural elements, role prescriptions, and reward structures, as suggested by the normative-reeducative strategy described by Chin and Benne (1969).

People Model

The opposite pole of our continuum of change strategies is the belief that organizational change is affected through revising the people variables rather than the structural variables. The variables in the people model are individual values, perception, communication skills, problem-solving abilities, conflict resolution skills, and a host of other interpersonal and group relations dynamics. The underlying assumption is that organizations are changed when values, attitudes, and individual competencies are changed; change the person, therefore, change the structure.*

Argyris (1964) contends that the needs of the organization (structure) and the needs of people are diametrically opposed. He assumes that individuals strive for independence and awareness of and control over self as adults accompanied by a sense of integrity and self-worth. But organizations strive to increase quality and quantity of output, to keep personnel dependent because of the chain of command, and to create situations requiring dependence and passivity. The resolution of this dilemma, according to Argyris, is to increase interpersonal competence which will result in the modification of technological (structural) factors.

Blake and Mouton (1969) address themselves to the issue of encouraging maximum concern for productivity along with maximum concern for people throughout the organization. This dual concern is implemented through a six-phase, three-year leadership training program. The first two phases deal with management development (reeducation and team building), and the last four phases deal with organizational change (interteam building, goal setting, implementation, and stabilizing change). But, though affecting structure is part of the grid approach, through the learning of openness, participation, and conflict resolution, "cognitive and attitudinal change is hypothesized to yield overall organizational change" (Tushman, 1974, p. 10). Team leadership and team building are people-oriented approaches to change that also affect the structure of an organization.

Team Leadership

Teams, like groups, are composed of individuals who interact with one another, and who must rely on that interaction for success and achievement of goals. In teams, effort is synergized so that the product, whatever it may be, takes on an importance greater than the sum of its parts.

Leadership is required to develop a team. Specifically, team leadership includes: (1) the development of individual leadership capabilities; (2) the development of skills necessary for effective group pro-

---

*There are many variations of the people approach, such as theories of needs (Maslow, 1954); planned change (Lippitt and others, 1958; Bennis and others, 1969); organizational renewal (Lippitt, 1969); and system-4 organization (Likert, 1967).

cess, that is, a sound grounding in concepts *and* practice of interpersonal and intergroup communication and process skills; and (3) the development and use of the "dynamic" that the leadership of any group may constantly shift to whichever individual has the necessary information and skills for the resolution of the issues or problems before the group (Buchtel and Guzzetta, 1977).

Team building emphasizes the advantages of participative problem solving and decision making as opposed to more traditional authoritarian decision making. Through a variety of methods, members of the team are helped to institute group processes more expertly, share information more openly, experience more group problem solving, establish more trust, develop more cohesiveness, and practice greater collaboration, all of which are seen as a positive contribution to a more effective and efficient group and, by implication, organizational functioning.

Considerable attention is being paid to developing the effectiveness of groups or teams because many modern organizations are extremely complex systems that can no longer be managed singlehandedly in the traditional "great president" mode. Problems must be solved through the efforts of people of diverse backgrounds, skills, and personalities.

In addition, the current trend toward matrix structure in many organizations underscores the need for team development. Typically, in the matrix structure, goals are achieved by establishing project task forces that operate for the life of the project and are then disbanded. As Bennis and others (1969) suggested a decade ago, the future key word for the structure of organizations would be "temporary"; that is, organizations would consist mainly of rapidly changing, temporary, problem-oriented task forces composed of strangers who represent a diverse set of professional skills. These temporary group members, from diverse units or disciplines, must be ready to develop positive group functions, maintain their own identity within the group, and accomplish a complex task. Creating an environment for the successful merging of a variety of talents and skills is the basic goal of team building.

The need for teams and, by inference, team leadership development, is stated succinctly by Maio and Buchtel (1977) as they discuss the mission of an urban university: "What the urban university needs is not a project director for urban studies, but a team of competent individuals who pool their respective academic and administrative competencies to design and implement programs. . . . The use of project teams, task forces, and other types of temporary systems will be the appropriate way for the university to optimize the different capabilities of its human resources" (p. 3). Appointing a task force or a committee is surely nothing new at universities. What is new is the recognition that groups of people need to be helped to know *how* to pool their competencies toward the accomplishment of a goal. The *how* is the essence of team building.

One might think that the time and effort involved in helping groups of people function effectively is not worth the time and trouble. Indeed, the use of a team is not always appropriate. For instance, team development may be contrary to a director's own philosophy; the work unit may not require collaborative action; or there may not be enough time to achieve a task using the team approach (Dyer, 1977). However, the traditional tension between faculty and administration suggests the value of the team approach to negotiate this tension, particularly in an era of dwindling resources when hard decisions need to be made with potentially high personal consequences for university personnel, administration, and faculty.

There are additional values working in the team or matrix mode. The knowledge explosion is so great that encompassing its totality is far beyond the capabilities of a single individual. Working together encourages consultation, that is, asking for and receiving needed expert information and advice from others. Because personal and work selves can never be fully separate, well-functioning teams frequently serve to fill basic human needs for security, status, esteem, and opportunity for growth and meaningful relationships.

Teams or work groups provide an arena in which new skills and behaviors can be tested, providing the environment and climate is such that the threat to status or personal sense of worth is minimized. Additionally, as information is shared in teams or work groups, the teams can become vehicles by which the understanding of and commitment to the organization can be enhanced. As people get a clearer idea of how their tasks relate to the goals of the organization and to the tasks of others around them, they are much more likely to accept those goals as their own.

Another benefit of team or work groups is their use in creating within organizations what is called a "critical mass." Change theorists suggest that in order to provide the necessary energy to initiate, implement, and maintain change, it is necessary to involve a significant number of people in the effort. Beckhard and Harris (1977) define that critical mass as those individuals or groups whose active support will ensure that the desired change will take place. Those particular individuals or groups will vary from organization to organization. In many instances, it will be management-level persons or groups, and initial team-building efforts are concentrated at that level. For other organizations, it may be more effective to build teams from a "diagonal slice" of the organization, that is, representatives of various functions, locations, levels and subgroups. Where to enter the organization (leverage) and how to join individuals or groups in networks (linkage) until a significant proportion of the organization has been affected are two critical decisions dependent upon the unique situation of individual organizations.

Teaching Team Leadership Skills. Once the decision has been made concerning the membership of the teams—top management, lower-level management, and heterogeneous groups representing the total organization—much time and effort must be expended on identifying the concepts to be included in team leadership development, teaching them in the most effective way, and choosing evaluation processes that will best measure the effectiveness of the team leadership development attempt.

The concepts included in a team leadership development program are those which are necessary to help individuals and groups develop their diagnostic and leadership skills for the purpose of applying them to identified needs within the organization. Such concepts include perception, listening, communication, problem solving, conflict management, decision making, and creativity. In addition, teams should be helped to understand the operations of the organization of which they are a part. This process includes emphasizing concepts such as various organizational structures, impact of differing leadership styles, motivation, and role functions. Finally, teams should become more aware of the impact of the environmental constraints on organizations and individuals. Although many leadership programs essentially adopt one of these three perspectives as their primary focus, all three perspectives are essential to a well-rounded program. Since an organization is best seen in a total systems sense, teams benefit from understanding the interrelatedness of the individual, group, and organizational structure in order to appreciate that change in any one of these areas will influence every other part of the system.

Change theorists suggest that change is best achieved if those affected by the change are involved in the planning process. Also learning is better achieved by providing a process by which team members can move from hearing conceptual materials to applying those materials to real situations in small groups that will encourage interactions, then moving back to reviewing the experience and sharing the learning as a total group. Such a procedure can help team members review past learning, consider and practice new learning, and anticipate future learning.

Difficult though it may be to plan and carry out, an evaluation component for a team leadership development program is essential. Evidence supporting the success or failure of programs must be gathered systematically and scientifically for effective decision making. Formative evaluation, that is, assessing the effectiveness of each aspect of the program, aids in modifying and improving subsequent efforts. Summative evaluation, that is, assessing the overall effectiveness and impact of the program, can help determine how the program is affecting organizational function and structure, providing one more link between the people and structure change strategy models. Careful evaluations can in themselves provide for organizational self-renewal (Pomrenke, 1979).

Participative Decision Making. Creating new teams and the increasing use of teams in decision making raises the question of participative decision making. Although universities make a strong case for the ideal of democracy, equality of influence (power), and collegiality, the increasing tension on campuses nationwide indicates that perhaps the ideal and the real are still poles apart. Even when universities pay more than lip service to participative decision making, the procedures for bringing about the participation rarely go beyond elected or appointed committees. Pollay and others state: "Even the most enthusiastic of those politically committed to the fostering of participation in decision making have failed to generate any variety of means for realizing such participation" (1976, pp. 145–146). Participative decision making, however, is a sensitive issue in higher education. Universities have "high talent" personnel; that is, they include a large number of professionals. And where there are large numbers of professionals, there is a high probability of conflict because of the push-pull forces of organizational goals versus professional goals.

But participative decision making has more benefits than mere survival. Research on small groups indicates that people are likely to have a greater commitment to a decision and its implementation if they have been involved in making it; that participation increases the probability that more of the available informational and experiential resources will be used; that locating the decision more closely to the source of the problem generally results in a better decision; and that increased communication, a natural result of participative decision making, generally leads to more effective group performance (Katz and Kahn, 1978).

Some caveats, however, are in order. Participative decision making is not synonymous with pure democracy. Accountability and responsibility demand that the "buck stop somewhere," usually with the department head, dean, vice-president, and/or president. In other words, participation in decision making is not decision making. In addition, imposing participation on people not wishing to be involved is counterproductive. Participation is usually desired only when it affects one's work experience. Finally, some decisions need to be made on a unilateral level, using criteria such as the critical nature of the decision, the time constraints for making the decision, and the personnel who need to be involved in the decision. Such criteria can be used to judge the appropriateness of participative decision making. Caveats notwithstanding, acknowledging the benefits of wide participation in major decisions within a university as well as designing structures, policies, and procedures that will make participative decision making possible, appear to be useful for universities.

Transference of Learning. A crucial element of the people approach to organizational change is the issue of transference of learning. Although conceptual knowledge may be learned and even practiced in the training/workshop/seminar situation, it is frequently not applied and practiced in the work situation. For years, organizations have sent their directors or managers away for training, assuming they would be able to bring new insights to their own work groups. There is mounting evidence suggesting that the pressures of the work unit tend to overwhelm any efforts to change by the individual, even if he or she is in a supervisory position. Therefore, it is the work unit, not the director or manager alone, that should be exposed to alternative procedures for problem solving.

Some partial solutions for bridging the gap between learning and practice have been suggested. Training the entire work group, or at least a significant proportion of it, raises the probability that new behaviors will be considered, particularly if the trained group contains those individuals who tend to set the behavior norms for the group, and if an atmosphere has been created that minimizes the threat of acting in new and different ways.

Transference of learning will be enhanced if the learning situation focuses on problems that are real rather than hypothetical. This approach serves several purposes: Participants are helped to diagnose and gain insight into the dynamics of troublesome situations; they are encouraged to generate alternate solutions to the problems; and they have the opportunity to rehearse or "role play" solutions to the problems with the instructor or fellow participants providing supportive critiques. In this way, learning and the application of that learning are linked together in a way that encourages more "back-home" application and provides greater potential for long-range retention of the learning.

In addition to dealing with real situations in the training experience, transference of learning can be accelerated if the training design is such that the participants know they will be expected to apply newly acquired knowledge and skills to specific tasks within the organization. Argyris (1976, p. xii) states that "people design and solve problems differently if they know they will end their learning with understanding than if they know they will be asked to use their understanding to make events come about."

Transference of learning depends not only on effective planning within the training design but also on dynamics in the organization itself. In other words, what can the organization do to support the successful transfer and stabilization of change? The most effective element for encouraging application of new behavior is an organizational climate in which innovation and problem solving are encouraged and rewarded. The necessity for support from top management and/or influential organization members in order to accomplish change has been amply documented. It is these people who frequently set climate and have access to sources of reward. If they support and positively reinforce innovation, through both tangible and intangible rewards, there is a higher probability that innovative behavior will be practiced in the work situation.

Closely related to the notion of climate and reward for change is the need to widely disseminate information concerning change efforts throughout the organization. Not only does this practice reduce the possibility of misjudging the motives of change-oriented persons, but it also provides a feedback and information channel by which personnel in the total organization can assess their own situation in relation to changes in other parts of the system. Some procedures for achieving information and feedback channels are: calling meetings of significant campus groups for purposes of sharing information and soliciting response; providing written reviews through dissemination of minutes or summaries of planning meetings via house organs; establishing temporary advisory groups to encourage ideas from various parts of the system; and planning refresher or renewal follow-up training events in which participants can examine what has happened to them in the work situation.

A More Useful Theory of Change: Contingent and Integrated

In the literature in change theory, the advocates of each approach described here make convincing cases for the merit of their position. Structural-change theorists are convinced that the only way change can be initiated, implemented, and maintained is to reorganize functional units and/or readjust policies, procedures, and role expectations. It is clear, however, that shifts in role structure or redesigned relationships may lead to role conflict with a decrease in organizational effectiveness and an increase in individual tensions. People-change theorists are equally convinced that the only way change can be brought about is to provide individuals with new understandings and skills that will lead to more effective interpersonal and group dynamics. The first order of business, therefore, is to provide those understandings and skills through training or reeducation. There are, however, centers of power and entrenched structures in any organization, and, unless they are enlisted in the change effort, all the training in the world will not bring about organizational change.

Obviously, both positions have merit and are reasonable analyses of what it takes to bring about change. If this is true, the change agent is left with basically three approaches: (1) use either structural or the people approach; (2) use both approaches in sequence; (3) use both approaches in tandem. Given the experiences to date in organizational development, and the pros and cons of each approach as described in the literature, it would appear that the first approach should be eliminated.

In the second approach, one is confronted with the question of sequence. When is it better to begin the change effort by focusing on structure, and when is it better to begin the change effort by focusing on people? Tushman (1974) hypothesizes that the degree of predictability of the task or goal is the critical variable in determining whether to enter the system with a structural or a people approach. His analysis of a glass-producing plant suggests that in an organization of that nature the task is clear and concrete, and information needed for decision making is concentrated in the upper levels of the organization. He concludes that for such an enterprise, the best sequence for change is the structural approach followed by the people approach.

Universities, however, bear little resemblance to a glass-producing plant. The task or goal in universities, that of producing an educated individual, is exceedingly complex. Furthermore, in universities, information needed for decision making is concentrated not in administrative ranks but in faculty ranks. Perhaps more accurately, it is concentrated in both areas. Where significant decisions are made is frequently a matter of debate and controversy, and often claimed by faculty under the banner of academic freedom. For such an enterprise, following Tushman's views, the best sequence for change is the people approach followed by the structural approach. That is to say, individuals and groups of people become the prime targets for change efforts.

Lippitt and others (1958, p. 139) make a similar point in discussing the choice of a leverage point, "the keystone of the whole change process." Should the change agent enter the system through persons or subgroups or through the structural or functional component that most likely will lead to the change goal? They suggest that two criteria govern the choice of leverage. First, accessibility—where in the organization will the change effort most likely take hold? Second, linkage—where in the organization is the highest likelihood that the change effort will progress or "ripple through" to the areas that one hopes to affect by the change?

The concept of linkage leads to a discussion of the second characteristic of a university approach to change, namely integration. An integrated change strategy means that, as much as possible, both targets of the change effort—people and structure—be approached in tandem and be functionally integrated.

Although the following point should not be used to rationalize little or ineffective preplanning with regard to change efforts, networking or linkage opportunities frequently emerge from the change activities themselves. For instance, some networks may not have been envisioned or even deemed possible until unanticipated contacts emerging from the program pave the way. On the negative side, new adversary groups (participants in a change effort versus nonparticipants) may emerge from a change effort. Those who plan change need to be constantly alert, flexible, and able to turn serendipitous happenings into positive contributions to change efforts.

The approach to change being suggested is no easy matter. Universities are very difficult to analyze and diagnose (as are most complex organizations). Decisions regarding leverage and linkage are complicated and intricate. Because of the fluid nature of change efforts, the following questions may provide some basic guidelines for planning change efforts.

- What is the mission and purpose (product) of the university?
- What environmental constraints are impinging on the university?

- At what level is relevant information necessary for more effective functioning?
- Where should the locus of decision making be lodged for greatest efficiency and effectiveness?
- Should the locus of decision making vary, depending on the level of decision needs?
- Which change sequence is most appropriate for the university and for subgroups within the university?
- Where is the most accessible entry point for the change effort?
- Is upper level administration supportive of the change efforts?
- What channels are available to communicate changes to the total university?
- What components would best form the network of change, and how can they be linked, maintained, and nurtured?
- How can the university personnel be involved and their skills increased to implement change efforts?
- Is there credible evidence that the changes will produce results that will be congruent with the values and desires of university personnel?
- Is the change plan comprehensive enough to include individual, group, and organizational needs? (Lindquist, 1978, pp. 231-233)

This list of questions is surely not exhaustive. A greatly augmented list, more precisely suitable for individual universities, could be generated by a representative group of university personnel in a relatively short brainstorming session.

Change, particularly change that can be accomplished through team leadership with attention to both structural and people variables, can and should be deliberately planned and based on sound principles. The implementation of that change, however, involves many factors that cannot be fully known in advance, and, even if they could be anticipated, might not be controllable. One is left then with the need to remain flexible, adaptable, and alert. Although a certain amount of "seat-of-the-pants" artistry is still necessary, one does have enough knowledge and can acquire skills toward a more realistic engineering of change, moving toward a state of affairs that is more desirable than that which now exists.

References

Argyris, C. *Integrating the Individual and the Organization.* New York: Wiley, 1964.
Argyris, C. *Increasing Leadership Effectiveness.* New York: Wiley, 1976.
Baldridge, J. V. *Power and Conflict in the University.* New York: Wiley, 1971.
Beckhard, R., and Harris, R. T. *Organizational Transitions: Managing Complex Change.* Reading, Mass.: Addison-Wesley, 1977.

Bennis, W. G., Benne, K. D., and Chin, R. (Eds.). *The Planning of Change*. New York: Holt, Rinehart and Winston, 1969.

Blake, R. T., and Mouton, J. S. *Building a Dynamic Organization Through Grid Organization Development*. Reading, Mass.: Addison-Wesley, 1969.

Buchtel, F. S., and Guzzetta, D. J. "The W. K. Kellogg Foundation Program for the Development of Team Leadership at The University of Akron." In *Proceedings*, Academic Administrative Workshops, Ninth Annual Conference, American Institute of Decision Sciences, Chicago, October 19, 1977.

Chin, R., and Benne, K. D. "General Strategies for Effecting Changes in Human Systems." In W. G. Bennis, K. D. Benne, and R. Chin (Eds.), *The Planning of Change*. New York: Holt, Rinehart and Winston, 1969.

Deep, S. *Human Relations in Management*. Encino, Calif.: Glencoe, 1978.

Dyer, W. G. *Team Building: Issues and Alternatives*. Reading, Mass.: Addison-Wesley, 1977.

Hersey, P., and Blanchard, K. *Management of Organizational Behavior*. Englewood Cliffs, N.J.: Prentice-Hall, 1972.

Kahn, R. L. "Organizational Development: Some Problems and Proposals." In J. M. Ivancevich, A. D. Szilagyi, Jr., and M. J. Wallace, Jr. (Eds.), *Readings in Organizational Behavior and Performance*. Santa Monica, Calif.: Goodyear, 1977.

Katz, D., and Kahn, R. L. *The Social Psychology of Organizations*. New York: Wiley, 1978.

Leavitt, H. "Applied Organizational Change in Industry." In J. March (Ed.), *Handbook of Organizations*. Chicago: Rand McNally, 1965.

Lefrancois, G. R. *Psychology for Teaching*. Belmont, Calif.: Wadsworth, 1979.

Likert, R. *The Human Organization*. New York: McGraw-Hill, 1967.

Lindquist, J. *Strategies for Change*. Berkeley, Calif.: Pacific Soundings Press, 1978.

Lippitt, G. *Organizational Renewal*. New York: Appleton-Century-Crofts, 1969.

Lippitt, R., Watson, J., and Westley, B. *The Dynamics of Planned Change: A Comparative Study of Principles and Techniques*. New York: Harcourt Brace Jovanovich, 1958.

Maio, E. A., and Buchtel, F. S. "The Importance of Team Leadership Development to the Urban University's Mission." Paper presented at the National Invitational Conference, "Toward the Urban University," Northeastern Illinois University, Chicago, May 9-10, 1977.

Maslow, A. H. *Motivation and Personality*. New York: Harper & Row, 1954.

Pollay, R. W., Taylor, R. N., and Thompson, M. "A Model for Horizontal Power Sharing and Participation in University Decision Making." *Journal of Higher Education*, 1976, *47*, 141-157.

Pomrenke, V. "Program Evaluation: Three Problem Areas." The Selected Paper Series, Organizational Development Division, American Society for Training and Development, Madison, Wisconsin, 1979.

Tushman, M. *Organizational Change: An Exploratory Study and Case History*. ILR Paperback No. 15. Ithaca: New York State School of Industrial and Labor Relations, Cornell University, 1974.

"W. K. Kellogg Foundation Program for the Development of Team Leadership at an Urban University, Final Report: January 1976–February 1978." Akron, Ohio: The University of Akron, 1978.

Velma Pomrenke is a research associate with The University of Akron Team Leadership Development Program. She is coordinator of the Program for the Development of a Model Network of University/Community Team Leadership, a project sponsored by the W. K. Kellogg Foundation.

*After institutional goals and objectives have been established,
it is not very difficult to identify those that impinge upon
the knowledge and skills of faculty and administrators.*

Faculty and Administrative Development

G. Melvin Hipps

Since higher education is what is often referred to as a "labor-intensive industry," it stands to reason that developing the workers in the industry ought to be one of the major goals in any program designed to bring about change. Although the concept of professional growth of faculty and administrators in colleges and universities is hardly a novel one, the phrases "faculty development" and "administrative development" are relatively new to the argot of higher education. They refer to structured programs that assist college faculty and administrators in developing the knowledge and skills necessary for improving their performances in their several roles and to assist them in providing for continuous personal and institutional renewal. Faculty and administrative development programs share many of the same goals, objectives, and activities and are thus frequently referred to in this chapter under the umbrella term *professional development.* There is some evidence that programs for faculty and programs for administrators are being combined. Charles Farmer (1979) has suggested that faculty development centers be expanded or reorganized to include administrators.

College faculty and administrators have traditionally been produced through on-the-job training; if they became good at their jobs,

G. Hipps (Ed.). *New Directions for Institutional Research: Effective Planned Change Strategies,* no. 33.
San Francisco: Jossey-Bass, March 1982.

they did so by the trial-and-error approach and through the good office of kindly, benevolent, and experienced colleagues who had themselves been educated in the proverbial "school of hard knocks." These methods, combined with whatever natural talent and intelligence had been bestowed upon one at birth, were considered (and still are by many) to be the only route to success in college teaching or administration. Of course it was assumed that the teacher would be well-grounded in his or her discipline, and that there was an invariable positive correlation between knowledge in one's field and competence in teaching. It was also assumed that the only relevant prerequisite for the would-be administrator was a successful career as a teacher.

Until the advent of the faculty development movement, the approaches to professional growth and development were the traditional sabbatical leave, allowances for attendance at professional meetings, and grants for research and publication. Since faculty members viewed themselves as chemists or historians or literary critics who happened to make their living by teaching, and since advancement was determined by the recognition of one's scholarly achievements by one's professional peers, the sabbatical, the research grant, and attendance at the meetings of one's professional society were the logical faculty development activities to receive institutional support. Although a few scattered colleges had sabbatical programs for administrators (and there are still apparently very few), the major support for administrative development was, and still is, a travel allowance for attendance at conferences on higher education and a budget for pertinent literature on college administration.

When one contemplates the process of planning change through faculty and administrative development, the foremost reality to be confronted is that there are no short-cuts to the design and implementation of a program that will bring about significant changes in people and thus in institutions. Unfortunately, many development programs established during the past decade have been ad hoc arrangements, supported more often than not by soft money and tolerated by the faculty and administration because of the external grants brought in to support them.

Before considering the process of planning a faculty and administrative development program, it might be helpful to examine some counterproductive strategies for getting such a program underway. The first one is the importation of a program from another school. There are three problems with this approach. One, it short-circuits the planning process that is essential to the potential success of the program. Two, it tends to alienate the faculty and administrators who quite naturally feel they can devise a program that is as effective as that of any other school. Third, it falsely assumes that there is *a* program model that is appropriate in any set of circumstances.

A second counterproductive strategy is designing a program to suit the guidelines of an agency that provides funding for faculty and administrative development. If the interests of the agency and the goals of the institution do not coincide, then both the agency and the institution are destined to be frustrated and disappointed. Furthermore, a program that begins by this strategy, even if it is successfully carried out during the period of the grant, is not likely to be continued when the external funding has been exhausted.

A development program introduced by administrative fiat is a third strategy to avoid. Although administrators might need to provide the necessary strong leadership to get a program underway, it is probably fatal for an administrator unilaterally to install a development program, even one for administrators. However obvious the need for a program may be, and however pessimistic an administrator may be about getting the faculty to plan a program that will address real needs, it is at best a waste of time and at worst a serious blow to faculty morale and initiative for an administrator to mandate a program.

Finally, one should avoid establishing a development program with an inappropriate link to the institutional evaluation system. One of the major influences on the faculty and administrative development movement has been the drive for accountability and the consequent shifting of approaches to evaluation. Sadly, the negative aspects of this shift have constituted a formidable obstacle to the acceptance of development programs by faculty and administrators. Although writers in the field of professional development differ in their views of the proper relationship of evaluation and development, most agree that development programs are damaged if not destroyed when the primary motivation for participation in them is the stick of evaluation rather than the carrot of instrinsic and extrinsic rewards. Furthermore, most staff members in professional development centers feel their effectiveness would be seriously impaired if they were perceived to have a formal or informal role in the institutional evaluation process.

If program importation, administrative fiat, grantsmanship programming, and remedial programming based on negative evaluations are counterproductive strategies for planning change through professional development, what are some productive ones? The strategies for planning such programs described in this chapter are drawn primarily from a management-by-objectives model. The selection of this model may appear to emphasize the rational approach to change while ignoring the emotional, social, and political ramifications of change. Jack Lindquist (1978c) has correctly identified one of the problems of professional development programs as being a failure to combine the various strategies for change, which he labels rational planning, social interacting, human problem solving, and political approaches. However, one must decide on some organizing principle or course of action that will allow for implementing and integrating all of these approaches. Since colleges are made up of people who view themselves as solving problems by rational analysis, perhaps the rational model is an appropriate context for planning a professional development program for a college.

The first step in the planning of institutional change through faculty and administrative development is the formulation of and general agreement on the institutional mission and on institutional goals and objectives. These must be sufficiently specific to suggest the place of faculty and administrative development in carrying out the mission of the school. Without adequate planning at this stage, all else is futile. Institutions that come out strongly in support of excellence in teaching in this mission statement and then give all the rewards, both real and psychological, to research and publication are creating a completely untenable foundation for a faculty development program. Administrators who sell programs for nontraditional students to students, parents, and legislators while the faculty goes on planning and implementing programs exclusively for traditional students are setting the stage for disillusionment on the part of everyone. These are only two examples that illustrate the impossibility of discussing the development of faculty and administrators until it has been determined *what they are being developed to do*. Arriving at a statement of mission and goals and objectives requires careful surveying of the opinions of the college's various constituencies, a study of the institution's environment, an honest assessment of its strengths and weaknesses, the setting of priorities, and an analysis of resources necessary for carrying out the mission.

After institutional goals and objectives have been established, it is not very difficult to identify those that impinge upon the knowledge and skills of faculty and administrators. With these as guides, an institution is ready to begin the next step in the process, assessing the needs of faculty and administrators in order for them to fulfill their own professional goals and to accomplish what the institutional goals require of them. Needs assessment, like institutional goal setting, is not a simple one-step process accomplished by distributing a questionnaire containing all the development activities the questionnaire maker can think of. A survey of needs of this sort may be a useful device, but it is not the only useful one and is probably not the first one that should be employed.

If the typical faculty member were asked what he needed in the way of professional development, he or she would doubtless reply, "More financial support for travel, research, and publication and relief from some of the burdens of teaching and advising that prevent these activities." Some education, therefore, appears to be necessary as a preliminary stage to a formal needs assessment. Although the possibility exists that this period of "education" may be viewed by some as a manipulation of the needs analysis to create needs where none exist, it must be admitted that it is designed to deal with the "no problem" problem, to provide activities that will lead to self-analysis, and to raise the level of consciousness of faculty and administrators to the possibilities for their development.

Explorations into the trends and issues in higher education and into the nature of teaching and learning and a few engaging and convincing demonstrations of alternative approaches to teaching and advising are helpful in broadening one's perspective on professional development. These activities may take the form of workshops, seminars, retreats, encounter groups, or whatever; the point is that such explorations, discussions, and demonstrations should be viewed as part of the needs assessment and not as the program for development. These preliminary events help to filter out unproductive ideas and program formats, to bring into focus productive ideas and approaches, and to validate the intellectual respectability of discussion centering on teaching and learning as opposed to a particular discipline.

Another stage of the needs assessment process that is very productive is scheduling private interviews with large numbers of faculty and administrators. These should be conducted by faculty members or administrators respected for their ability and noted for their discretion. The purposes of such interviews are to explore in some depth the specific concerns about professional development of individuals who might be unwilling or unable to share these concerns in another context and to allow them to analyze their own strengths and needs. Too often needs assessments ignore this step of personal analysis, probably because it can be disquieting and time consuming. However, asking people to enumerate their needs without first analyzing their strengths and weaknesses and coming to grips with what they can change and are willing to change renders the needs assessment irrelevant.

Finally, one or more questionnaires or surveys designed to elicit needs in professional development are no doubt useful in rounding out the process of needs assessment. If these are based on the common experiences in the first two stages of the process described here, as opposed to being lifted from some other institution's questionnaire, they can provide meaningful data on which to base program planning. If there are individuals who could not share their real concerns in the private interviews, the questionnaires should contain an open-ended section where their concerns can be noted. The process described here could take a year or more if it were properly carried out.

The next stage in planning change through faculty and administrative development is designing goals and objectives for a development program. These should naturally flow from the needs assessment, which flows from the institutional goals and objectives. This stage in the process should be viewed as two-pronged. Individual faculty and administrators should establish their own goals and objectives for their personal and professional development based on their own needs assessment and on the institutional needs assessment. Likewise, the goals and objectives for the professional development program should be based on the needs assessment of individuals as well as the collective needs assessment of the institution. Without this merging of individual and institutional interests, a professional development program is likely to be fragmented and inconsequential.

It is in the stages of developing needs assessments and goals and objectives that program planning most often goes awry. It is too tempting to jump into a whirlwind of activities before deciding what can and should be changed through a professional development program, how best to go about effecting change, in what time frame change can and should occur, and how to recognize desirable change when it has taken place.

The next stage is planning the actual program. Although budget has not been mentioned before, budgetary considerations must pervade the entire process of program planning, especially in these days of economic tribulations. Presumably, a general commitment has been made to faculty and administrative development in the period of setting institutional goals and objectives and of setting goals and objectives for a development program. Certainly one cannot have goals that involve allocation of financial resources without having resources to commit or without being willing to commit resources that are available. But at this point, the commitment has to be made specific so that a program can be planned within budgetary limitations. Since external funding for faculty and administrative development is largely a thing of the past, institutions are rapidly coming to the moment of truth when real commitment to professional development is about to be tested. Even if external money were available, many people involved in development programs would argue that unless an institution is willing to commit hard dollars to such programs, it would be best not to begin a program at all. In order to ensure a fair share of the budget for professional development, some schools have begun to allocate a certain percentage of the instructional budget to development activities.

Because so much external money has been available for professional development, faculty and administrators have lost sight of the fact that a creditable development program need not cost a great deal of money. There is sufficient expertise on most campuses to provide worthwhile development activities without a large professional staff or outside consultants. Faculty and administrators can learn a great deal from each other if they are willing to develop the necessary collaborative skills.

Once the budgetary limitations are known, the structure of the program can begin to take shape. As this stage of planning proceeds, there are certain principles that should be kept in mind. First, faculty must have a sense of ownership of any faculty development program, and administrators must own an administrative development program. This does not mean that there is no involvement or collaboration of faculty and administrators in designing programs for the two groups. Administrators may take the lead in getting a faculty development program underway; similarly, faculty may take the lead in pressing for an administrative development program. Furthermore, each group may help "educate" the other concerning their development needs and may assist in the formulation of goals and objectives of programs for the other group. But the actual implementation and administration of a program should be primarily the responsibility of the group that the program is designed to serve. This is not to say, however, that there should be two separate and distinct programs. As was pointed out earlier, since many of the goals of faculty and administrative development programs are the same, and since faculty and administrative team building is essential in any workable scheme of participatory management, there is no reason why the needs of faculty and administrators cannot be served by a single development center.

The second principle to keep in mind in structuring a professional development program is that although faculty and administrators should own their development programs, other groups should be involved in them, notably students and trustees. Since the enhancement of the education experience of students is one of the major purposes of a college, any program for improvement of teaching or administration that does not include appropriate participation by students is likely to have its effectiveness considerably diminished. Such participation is valuable not only because of the insights students have to offer in designing a program, but also because it is an extremely worthwhile educational experience for students to engage in dialogue with faculty and administrators about the problems of teaching, learning, and administration. Furthermore, since it is sometimes difficult to convince trustees of the necessity of spending money on the professional development of faculty and administrators, it is therefore wise to include them in the planning process.

In the third place, program planners should anticipate, recognize, and seek to minimize resistance to the change sought through a program of faculty and administrative development. If the discussions and other activities related to needs assessment and goals and objectives have been sufficiently broad and have involved all the appropriate individuals, resistance at the point of program initiation ought to be lessened, though it will probably never be entirely eliminated. There are several causes of resistance to professional development programs. The intellectual grounding of most development programs in pedagogical, managerial, and organizational theories has been a stumbling block to many academicians. The impossibility of arriving at a formula for effective teaching or of describing the skills necessary for the administrator is another cause of resistance to development programs. Regardless of the possible advantages of a development program, many are bothered by adding what they see as a new bureaucratic layer on the organizational chart and thus a new line item in the budget. One of the most difficult obstacles to overcome is the all too frequent view of development programs as remedial measures for incompetents. Another fear is that activities related to instructional and organizational development will be supported at the expense of discipline-oriented research and publication.

Some strategies that may help to reduce resistance are involvement of respected, influential, and unquestionably competent individuals in the program; proving that fears and anxieties about such things as hidden agendas for evaluation are unfounded; guaranteeing that traditional development activities are not to be abandoned; and making certain that early activities are designed to produce immediately useful and satisfying results.

A fourth principle to be considered as a program is being initiated is that participation in the program must involve extrinsic as well as intrinsic rewards. Unless the development program is tied to the real, as well as the published, institutional reward system, it will simply be a line item in the budget that might as well be reallocated. If it is made clear what is expected of faculty members and administrators, and if they are given support for their professional development, then they must be rewarded as well as held accountable for improving their performance.

In setting up the actual structure of a professional development program, there are several issues that must be considered. One is whether there are to be certain persons from the faculty or administration assinged part time to administer the program. Jack Lindquist (1978b) argues that a center with a small but full-time staff and a small part-time professional or auxiliary staff is the most appropriate organization. This organizational structure demonstrates a high level of institutional commitment to the program. Furthermore, the professional development program is too important and too time consuming to be administered by those who have other demanding responsibilities and whose other duties may constitute a conflict of interest with the program.

Another issue is where the program will be placed in the institutional organization chart. Again, Lindquist (1978b) feels that the administration of such a program should answer to the highest possible administrative official so as to indicate the significance of the program, and that the director of the program should occupy a staff rather than a line position. A third issue is the nature and structure of the policy board for the program. If it is a committee, the selection process and make-up of the committee must be decided. The relationship of the policy board to the program administration must be clarified. A fourth issue, which gets into the area of program activities, has to do with a decision about whether services will be available to all and provided to those who ask for them on an individual client basis or whether services and group activities of a general nature will be provided for everyone. It is of course possible and perhaps desirable to do both.

The next stage in program planning is designing the program components and strategies. The components of a professional development program will obviously flow from the needs assessment and goals and objectives. Jerry Gaff (1975) has labeled the components of an instructional improvement program as faculty development, in which he includes personal growth and increased skill and knowledge related to teaching; instructional development, which he equates with curriculum development; and organizational development, which has to do with improving interpersonal relationships and group process. Bergquist's and Phillip's (1975) analysis of the aspects of a faculty development program includes instructional development, which is concerned with teaching strategies and learning styles; organizational development, which deals with team building, decision making, and managing conflict; and personal development, which emphasizes interpersonal relations. Nelsen (1979) has divided faculty development activities into four major categories: professional development, which includes broadening one's scholarly areas and improving research skills; instructional development, which concerns improving teaching skills and learning new skills; curricular change, which has to do with creating and revising courses; and organizational change, which involves setting new campus goals and developing organizational structures to facilitate faculty development.

If one combined the components discussed by Gaff, Bergquist and Phillips, and Nelsen, the list would consist of five categories of development activities: instructional development, curriculum development, organizational development, personal development, and professional development. The growing body of literature on this subject suggests that a comprehensive program would involve attention to all of these components, although program emphases may vary from campus to campus. It is in each of these areas that a professional development program would be expected to bring about changes.

Although the studies by Gaff, Bergquist and Phillips, and Nelsen deal with faculty development, the program components discussed in them would be appropriate for a professional development program for both faculty and administrators. Administrators might be more concerned with personal, organizational, and professional development than with other components, but they should also be involved in activities related to curricular and instructional development.

The following are a few examples of goals that are often adopted for an instructional development program: ways of gauging the effectiveness of an advising program, approaches to dealing with marginally prepared students, methods for matching teaching and learning styles, means of expanding the repertory of teaching and learning modes, and procedures for anticipating and identifying students' personal and academic problems and providing appropriate intervention. There are of course many strategies available in an instructional development strand of a faculty development program. Workshops on methods of teaching, developing instructional materials, evaluation of student learning, and using educational technology; seminars on learning theory and educational philosophy; consultative services for individual faculty, such as analysis of classroom philosophy; consultative services for individual faculty, such as analysis of classroom teaching and recommendations for improvement; release time to develop a new teaching technique; opportunities for new and experienced faculty to work together in mentor-novice relationships; and discussions involving faculty, students, and administrators to exchange views about productive and unproductive activities designed to enhance learning — these are but a few examples of activities in an instructional development program.

Those institutions that have grappled with the issues and strategies enumerated here have learned that a well-conceived and well-planned instructional development program is much more than an occasional workshop on leading discussions or using the opaque projector. Although there may be some occasions when one session is sufficient, the "one-shot" workshop on a complex topic, skill, or issue is probably a waste of time and money. Furthermore, any development activity, whether short-term or long-term, must be accompanied by appropriate follow-through activities. Nothing is more likely to kill a professional development program than the conclusion on the part of the participants that nothing ever comes of it.

Another component of a development program is curricular reform. This does not mean, as some have assumed, gathering political support to drop requirements that are unpopular with students. Nor does it mean adopting trendy courses or new vocational or professional courses. Nor does it necessarily involve developing interdisciplinary courses, individualized activities, or any other of the fashionable innovations of the last few years. These may be among the results of curricular reform, but lasting reform must be more pervasive than the adoption of the latest educational fad.

True curricular reform — that which should be the focus of a faculty and administrative development program — is an arduous and time-consuming process that begins at the same place professional development programs begin, namely, with a debate and then a consensus on the mission of the institution. It is a truism to say that a college cannot long continue if there is no convergence of its stated mission and its educational program. Next, faculty and administrators must explore in depth those other factors that govern the nature of the curriculum, that is, the needs, interests, and abilities of the students to be served; the needs and interests of the society to be served; and finally, the structure and sequence of knowledge in the various disciplines.

Curriculum reform, however, cannot stop with consensus on institutional mission and understanding of the determinants of the curriculum. It entails seeing to it that every course has goals and objectives consonant with those of the institution and the particular program of which it is a part, that the activities and teaching methods are appropriately chosen to achieve the objectives, and that the evaluation procedures measure student achievement based on the objectives. Furthermore, all of such planning should be done in advance and explained to students before a course begins. To those who are familiar with and sympathetic to this approach to curriculum planning, these suggestions may seem self-evident. To those who are averse to this kind of planning, the ideas may appear pedestrian and limiting, even a violation of academic freedom. But there is simply no substitute for having faculty and administrators ponder the issues of what is worth knowing or doing, how they know it is worth knowing or doing, and how one best comes to know and to do these things.

The activities or strategies available for curricular reform are similar to those in instructional development. As a matter of fact, instructional development and curricular development are not distinguished in many programs. One strategy, the value of which has been amply demonstrated, is the internal minigrant made available to a faculty member who wishes to engage in some aspect of innovative curriculum development. Putting grants of this sort on an equal basis with grants for research and publication will go a long way toward making curriculum development as respectable an activity as research.

The third major thrust of faculty and administrative development is improvement in the organizational structure and operations of the institution. The movement toward faculty participation in institutional governance has created a new need in professional development programs. If faculty members are to participate appropriately in the management of the college, they must have opportunities to acquire knowledge and skill in such areas as group dynamics, management of conflict and stress, needs assessment, resource allocation, and program evaluation. If faculty and administrators are to collaborate in institutional development, they must understand their own perceptions and the perceptions of others regarding their roles, and they must be adept at team building. Faculty members need to understand and appreciate various administrative styles and to develop the skill and flexibility necessary to work with different kinds of administrators. Administrators need to understand and appreciate the various types of personalities on the faculty, to accept their foibles as well as their virtues, and to learn what motivates each one to do his or her best work. Even in institutions where participative management is not the model for the total institutional operation, faculty members need assistance in improving their contributions in those areas in which they ordinarily have primary concern; for example, as committee members or chairpersons of such committees as curriculum, admissions, and library.

Another aspect of organizational development is the training of faculty members who have the ability and inclination to become administrators. If administrators continue to come from the ranks of the faculty, they can be given experiences that will get them ready for their new roles and will lessen the frustration inherent in on-the-job training. Since the position of departmental chairperson is traditionally the first job for the would-be administrator, and since departmental chairpersons are more and more being given managerial responsibilities, a professional development program could certainly provide training of this group. Like other administrators, they should no longer be expected, or indeed allowed, to learn by trial and error.

There are many strategies available for organizational development, depending on an institution's goals in this area. A college might wish to hire an outside consultant to study the organizational structure and make recommendations that would lead to greater efficiency, openness, communication, and collegiality. Workshops on such topics as management of time, group process in committees, role perceptions, and conducting meetings might be planned for faculty and administrators. Training sessions might be held for administrators and prospective administrators, including department chairpersons, on such topics as budget making, personnel policies, evaluation of personnel, planning the use of instructional support services, and so on.

Attendance at national conferences, seminars, and workshops has been idenfitied as one of the more prevalent strategies for professional development, especially for administrators. However, Jack Lindquist (1978a) points out that many programs for administrators are now emphasizing local, ongoing activities as those most likely to bring about lasting change. The reason for this emphasis is the realization that administrative development cannot be separated from the particular character and needs of the institution, and that carry-over of ideas from national off-campus programs is often quite minimal.

As was pointed out earlier, organizational development will probably be a major concern in any administrative development program. Boyer and Grasha (1978) have categorized the strategies available in administrative development programs under the following headings: (1) resource materials, (2) informational workshops and training, (3) short-term consultation: crisis, (4) short-term consultation: development, and (5) long-term consultation: development. The purposes and activities for the first three categories are fairly obvious. The fourth one, short-term consultation: development, addresses a particular task or project, such as recruiting, evaluation of teaching, or admissions. Long-term consultation: development deals with system redesign in such areas as curriculum, committee structure, and by-laws.

Personal development is the fourth program component in faculty and administrative development programs. This component might be interpreted broadly to include any activity to assist in the personal growth of a member of the faculty or administration. If this concept of personal development is the one adopted in a professional development program, then personal development activities will probably be indistinguishable from instructional, curricular, organizational, or professional development activities. However, if personal development is viewed more specifically in relationship to the problems individuals face throughout their careers, then some issues that may be pertinent are dealing with mid-career crisis, long-range career planning, retirement planning, career transitions, dealing with professional disappointments, value clarification, and resolution of personal crises brought on by such events as illness, divorce, or death of a loved one. Apparently not many programs deal with these issues directly.

A professional development program that includes the concept of personal development described here might adopt several approaches, again depending on the goals of the program and the resources available. There might be a counseling program for faculty and administrators to provide support during times of personal and professional crisis. There might be preretirement seminars. For faculty and administrators who are experiencing professional "burn-out," or who feel the need for "real world" experiences, there might be opportunities to work for a time in a job outside education. These kinds of activities bring up a problem that is present but not as acute in other program components, that is, the attitude that availing oneself of these services is an admission of a weakness or a deficiency that may be best concealed.

The fifth and final component of a faculty and administrative development program is professional development or renewal. The issues involved in this area are discovering ways of keeping up with and being enthusiastic about an academic discipline, finding time for research and publication, refining research skills, developing sources of financial assistance for research and for professional travel, and creating and maintaining relationships that provide intellectual stimulation in one's area of interest. The strategies available for this program component are the traditional ones — the sabbatical, research grants, and allowance for travel to professional meetings. Another strategy is an exchange program in which faculty and administrators are employed briefly in another institution. Because of the origins of the faculty development movement in instructional development, there may be a tendency to disparage or to take for granted these more traditional activities in professional development. Such an attitude would certainly feed the fears of faculty that the newer development programs are meant to supplant the traditional ones.

It should be stressed that all programs available in professional development should be equally accessible to both faculty and administrators. Many good administrators are lost because the only way they feel they can keep up in their disciplines is to return to the faculty. Furthermore, administrators who have developed innovative approaches to their administrative responsibilities may need to have the time and financial support to engage in professional activities, such as writing articles and books, speaking at conferences on higher education, and providing consulting services to other schools.

After considering program components and activities or strategies, program planners must turn finally to program evaluation. Without evaluation, all of the goal setting, needs assessment, and strategy planning will have been in vain because program planners will not know what worked, what did not work, and why. O'Connell and Meeth (1978) emphasize the importance of the goal-setting stage of program planning because if the goals are vague, ambiguous, or incomplete, the accomplishments of the program cannot be determined. In order to evaluate a professional development program, there must not only be a general agreement on program goals but also an agreement on what will constitute evidence of whether the goals have been accomplished. It should be clear, therefore, that the evaluation of a professional development program must be planned as part of the program and not tacked on as an afterthought.

Evaluation procedures need not, indeed must not, be cumbersome or excessively time consuming. However, such procedures must be comprehensive and systematic; comprehensive in that they attempt to measure the degree to which all goals and objectives have been achieved, and systematic in that they are employed at regular predetermined intervals and involve a variety of approaches. There should be a periodic review, perhaps annually, of program goals and objectives, an assessment of progress, and a reformulation of goals and objectives for the next year.

There is sometimes a tendency to confuse evaluation with gathering statistics on such things as number of workshops held, number of participants, number of visits to the development center, and so forth. While such data are invaluable in making one's case at budget-making time, they do not constitute a comprehensive evaluation program. Although formal evaluations involving questionnaires, structured interviews, observations, and statistical analyses of data are necessary and valuable, the more informal techniques such as open-ended interviews and case studies can be extremely helpful and revealing. Staff members charged with the responsibility of a professional development program must be constantly talking with faculty and administrators to find out what they are doing, what they want to do, how well the development program is assisting them in what they want to do, and how the program can better assist them in the future. Furthermore, the success story that can be embodied in a case study can be not only a convincing indicator of the quality of a development program but also a powerful motivator for participation in future development activities.

It should be obvious from the foregoing discussion that the process of bringing about change through faculty and administrative development programs is an extraordinarily complex operation. A program that is this intricate cannot be successfully mounted without careful and systematic planning. Further, a plan for a faculty and administrative development program is meaningless unless it exists within the framework of institutional development. Therefore, institutions that do not have a scheme for institutional planning are not yet ready to set up a professional development program. One may institute a series of workshops or seminars, but these do not constitute a program.

In concluding this chapter on faculty and administrative development, a word or two about "institutionalizing" development programs might be pertinent. A great deal has been written about institutionalization of development programs, especially those programs that were made possible by external funding. A preoccupation with institutionalization suggests that a program was begun without the knowledge, consent, or commitment of some significant group, and that this group must be lobbied relentlessly in order to win its support for continuation of a program. Although it would be naive to suggest that this kind of political activity is totally unnecessary, it is undeniably less important if a professional development program has been carefully and systematically planned; if there has been involvement and commitment of those for whom the program was planned; if this commitment has been evidenced by an appropriate allocation of time, money, and personnel; and if the program planned achieves its goals to a degree sufficient to warrant its continuation.

References

Bergquist, W. H., and Phillips, S. R. *A Handbook for Faculty Development.* Washington, D.C.: The Council for the Advancement of Small Colleges, 1975.

Boyer, R. K., and Grasha, A. F. "Theoretical Issues and Practical Strategies for Administrative Development." In J. A. Shtogren (Ed.), *Administrative Development in Higher Education.* Richmond, Va.: Higher Education Leadership and Management Society, 1978.

Farmer, C. H. *Administrator Evaluation: Concepts and Methods, Cases in Higher Education.* Richmond, Va.: Higher Education Leadership and Management Society, 1978.

Gaff, J. *Toward Faculty Renewal: Advances in Faculty, Instructional, and Organizational Development.* San Francisco: Jossey-Bass, 1975.

Lindquist, J. "Approaches to Administrative Development: A Synthesis." in J. A. Shtogren (Ed.), *Administrative Development in Higher Education.* Richmond, Va.: Higher Education Leadership and Management Society, 1978a.

Lindquist, J. *Designing Teaching Improvement Programs.* Berkeley, Calif.: Pacific Soundings Press, 1978b.

Lindquist, J. *Strategies for Change.* Berkeley, Calif.: Pacific Soundings Press, 1978c.

Nelsen, W. C. "Faculty Development: Key Issues for Effectiveness." *The Forum for Liberal Education, II,* October 1979.

O'Connell, W. and Meeth, R. L. *Evaluating Teaching Improvement Programs.* New Rochelle, N.Y.: *Change* Magazine, 1978.

G. Melvin Hipps, currently a writer and consultant in higher education, was formerly professor of education and English, associate academic dean, chairman, Department of Education, director of Graduate Studies, and coordinator of Programs for Faculty Development at Furman University. He was codirector of the Kellogg project at Furman.

*To have any success at all, a team leadership development
program would have to be a part of a total network of change.*

Case Study:
The University of Akron
Experience

Foster S. Buchtel

Colleges and universities, because they have taken on or been assigned
roles as enterprises and service agencies (Balderston, 1974) as well as
traditional educational institutions, often experience contradictory
expectations as they attempt to deal with problems in contemporary
society. The necessity to introduce institutional change and at the same
time to maintain a strong tradition of quality has forced institutions to
explore new organizational structures and management procedures.
Among the recent trends in higher education is a "new" form of organizational development, growing out of the conviction that neither our
past nor external forces affects our destinies and our ability to change
as much as does our increased awareness of "self" and "others." This
concept of organizational development moves from a focus on the individual to the institutional setting and emphasizes the merging of individual and institutional needs. This belief is deceptively simple in its
statement but confusingly complex in its implementation. Yet, it was
this philosophy that formed the basis for the team leadership development program at The University of Akron.

G. Hipps (Ed.). *New Directions for Institutional Research: Effective Planned Change Strategies*, no. 33.
San Francisco: Jossey-Bass, March 1982.

The University of Akron

Since its founding in 1870 as a church-related liberal arts college, The University of Akron has developed into a municipal university (1913) and then a state university (1967) with more than 23,000 credit and 5,000 noncredit students; nine degree-granting colleges plus an evening college, a university college, a graduate school, and a branch campus; thirteen doctoral programs; and two professional schools—law and nursing. In addition, the university has a consortium partnership in a medical school, public television, and graduate programs with two other universities. The University of Akron has a predominantly commuter student body and a 127-acre campus contiguous to the central business district of Akron. It enjoys the autonomy afforded by its own separate board of trustees, a sound fiscal base, and a healthy enrollment pattern.

Team Leadership: A Concept

All appears to be going well at The University of Akron, and the future looks promising. Why, then, a team leadership project aimed at facilitating change? The old way of looking at individual schools, departments, and administrative offices as autonomous, line and staff, separate, and with minimum interface is now being viewed by many as not useful for understanding and controlling the change process within a university. According to this view, persons within the university must understand and exploit the concept of matrix management (Sayles, 1976) as well as team leadership. The underlying principle of team leadership is that the leadership of any group is constantly shifting to whichever individual has the knowledge and skill necessary for the resolution of the issue before the group or organization (Buchtel and Guzzetta, 1977). The development of team leadership depends on the understanding and commitment to the group or the organizational goals; maximum use of the different resources of the individuals in the group; flexibility and sensitivity to the needs of others; development of group procedures to meet the particular problem or need; ability to examine the group and the organizational processes so as to continuously improve the team operation; establishment of appropriate steps and guidelines for decision making in the solution of problems; the development of trust and openness in communication and relationships; and a strong individual sense of belonging to the group or organization (Lippitt, 1969).

This was the theory. In application and practice, however, there were some problems. For example, how could we introduce the concept of team leadership into a complex network of more than 800 faculty members? And if we could, how could we be assured that the concepts would be converted into practice, and that the practice would be related to the improvement of the university and of the professional performance of individuals? How could we expect an activity that would be dealing primarily with the way things were done to have a lasting effect on the structure of the university? The answer is, we could not—if we dealt with team leadership development in isolation. To have any success at all in facilitating change, a team leadership development program would have to be part of a total network of change.

Why Team Leadership at The University of Akron?

The University of Akron has been fortunate in having strong presidential leadership throughout its history with the board of trustees carefully selecting the right president for the right time. This strong emphasis on the role of the president has helped the university reach its present status as the third largest, and one of the more diversified, universities in Ohio. But the "strong president" tradition also has its disadvantages. With few exceptions, this tradition has brought about a decline of the vitality of second- and third-level leaders within the university, individual upward and outward mobility, and a formal means of leadership development. It was recognized that one man at the helm could not be expected to provide all of the leadership needs of a complex organization striving to keep pace with social change, expectations, and demands, and, at the same time, maintain those traditions and programs that ensure a solid base of academic quality and credibility (Guzzetta, 1978). Thus, it was determined that the university should move toward the concept of functional or team leadership with the direction, motivation, recognition, and final decisions being provided by the "man at the top." This approach would require that the team leadership development program be a conscious part of a broader organizational plan aimed at producing appropriate change in the environment and in attitudes, along with the identification of potential leaders and the improvement of the leadership skills of both established and potential leaders.

A Network of Change

Although this case study will focus on the team leadership development program, it can best be understood within the context of the total "network of change" at the university. The major components of this network included: the two statements, "The Urban Mission of The University of Akron," and "Goals and Purposes of The University of Akron"; a commission on institutional planning and development; an institute for Futures Studies and Research; institutional research support; an Eduational Research and Development Center; interns and task forces resulting from the team leadership development project; and the Office of Team Leadership Development. Although these components were not established at the same time or in the sequence listed, they shared a common coordinating point in the Commission on Institutional Planning and Development. Further, all components of the network worked toward involving significant segments of the university in one or more of the basic elements of planned change: (1) systematic consideration of organizational goals and objectives; (2) identification of programs; (3) allocation of resources; (4) identification of priorities and alternatives; (5) program evaluation; (6) recognition of the importance of human values, objectives, and goals; (7) assistance given to the members of the organization in defining their purpose and the purpose of the organization; and (8) assisting the members of the organization to establish organizational norms consistent with the organizational goals (Buchtel, 1980; Michael, 1973; Ozbekhan, 1969; Ohio Board of Regents, 1973).

The Team Leadership Development Project

Although the basic objective of the team leadership development project was to prepare the faculty and administration to deal with the issues in all eight of the planned change elements, the primary focus of the program was helping individuals and teams deal with those described in numbers six, seven, and eight. It was also expected that the program would enlarge the pool of individuals who could become involved in the planning and decision-making process of the university. The goals and objectives of the two-year project funded by the W. K. Kellogg Foundation are summarized in Table 1.

The participants in the program were to be teaching faculty and administrators, approximately 830 persons at the time the project was conducted. A selection process was necessary because the project could accommodate only 100 to 120 participants for the initial phase of the program, the participants were expected to have demonstrated leadership potential, and the project design called for a horizontal (departments, divisions, and colleges) and vertical (position, rank, and status)

Table 1. The W. K. Kellogg Foundation Sponsored Program for the Development of Team Leadership at The University of Akron

Goals and Objectives

Goal	Objective
1. Identify individuals with leadership potential.	1. Increase the number of individuals within the University who are trained and involved in team leadership activities and who fall within a wide age grouping.
2. Raise their levels of motivation and dedication.	2. Increase the ratio of new appointments with team leadership potential and capabilities.
3. Develop teamwork and morale among these individuals.	3. Provide more visibility and greater rewards for those participating as positive members of the leadership team.
4. Further their individual development as leaders.	4. Develop a system of position descriptions and performance assessments to help in relating individual roles as a member of the team and to help in counseling toward improved participation.
5. Increase their readiness to accept change.	5. Improve participants' knowledge of the theory of leadership and its practice in the university setting and major reform movements and arguments in higher education.
6. Improve the quality of their decisions.	6. Improve participants' understanding of factors that influence individuals and groups, dynamics of organizations and change theory, basic concepts and practices of personal growth and leadership training, and his or her own needs, goals, motivations, and prejudices as a leader.
7. Establish a resource pool of leaders at various levels.	7. Improve participants' motivations and feelings toward a genuine desire to understand the needs, feelings, perceptions, goals, and problems of other people.
8. Improve the leadership capabilities of those already in key leadership positions.	8. Improve participants' capabilities to diagnose what is wrong when groups or organizations are not operating effectively, use procedures and methods that will be most effective in each situation, perform a variety of required leadership functions, evaluate and learn from his or her own experiences, and help others to improve their competencies as members and leaders.
9. Improve the total environment for leadership and change.	9. Develop a series of articles, papers, and monographs — conceptual, descriptive, and prescriptive — dealing with leadership development at an urban university.
10. Improve the leadership continuity needs of The University of Akron.	10. Establish the leadership development program as a continuing activity.

mix in each of the four classes. Although the selection process will be described later, it may be useful to cite the groupings used to help identify the "participant mix" in each class. The first two groupings of seven were faculty (rank and department mix) and staff/entry-level positions (department mix). The remaining five groups were:

Group A: The president and members of the executive group

Group B: Persons reporting to the vice-president and provost

Group C: Persons reporting to the vice-president and dean of student services

Group D: Persons reporting to the vice-president for planning, the vice-president for business and finance, and the executive director of university relations and development

Group E: Associates, assistants, and assistants to the deans; academic department and division heads.

The overall program design as originally conceived is depicted in Figure 1. Two activities that were added later were miniteam leadership workshops and team leadership breakfast forums. Following a description of the resource groups and the selection process, each of these steps will be discussed.

Resource Groups. A project director's advisory group and a program advisory group were appointed. The project director's advisory group was an informal group identified by the project director from faculty with demonstrated ability in the areas covered by the program. This group met weekly in the early stages of the project to provide theoretical and technical advice. A fourteen-member program advisory group, appointed by the president, included the chairman of the university board of trustees, the president (chairman), the project director (secretary), representatives of the major administrative areas, and representatives of the degree-granting colleges. This group provided guidance from the viewpoint of the members' constituencies. Subcommittees of the project advisory group were formed to select participants and interns after establishing the criteria for selection.

The Selection Process. During the first month of the project, a publicity campaign was launched through local newspapers, the campus/alumni newspaper, newsletters, and an all-faculty memorandum from the president. The president then sent letters to all faculty and administrators, inviting them to apply for the program and stressing its voluntary nature. Sufficient numbers of applications were received in response to this first invitation to fill all four classes. However, spaces were left available in classes III and IV to allow room for those who

Figure 1. Diagram of Team Leadership Development, Reinforcement, and Continuation

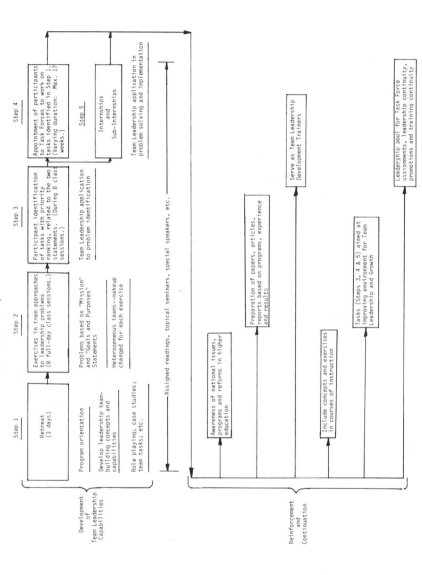

Step 1

Retreat (3 days)

Program orientation

Develop leadership team-building concepts and capabilities

Role playing; case studies; team tasks; etc.

Step 2

Exercises in team approaches to leadership problems (8 full-day class sessions.)

Problems based on "Mission" and "Goals and Purposes" Statements

Heterogeneous teams--makeup changed for each exercise

Step 3

Participant identification of tasks with priority ranking, related to the two statements. (During 8 class sessions.)

Team Leadership application to problem identification

Step 4

Appointment of participants to Task Forces to work on tasks identified in Step 1. (Varying duration: Max. 17 weeks.)

Step 5

Internships and Sub-Internships

Team Leadership application in problem solving and implementation

Development of Team Leadership Capabilities

Assigned readings, topical seminars, special speakers, etc.

Awareness of national issues, programs and reforms in higher education

Preparation of papers, articles, reports based on programs, experience and results

Serve as Team Leadership Development Trainers

Include concepts and exercises in courses of instruction

Tasks (Steps 3, 4 & 5) aimed at improving environment for Team Leadership and Growth

Leadership pool for Task Force assignments, leadership continuity, promotions and training continuity

Reinforcement and Continuation

might have taken a "wait and see" attitude. A second invitation to apply was sent out following the completion of the first class. A number of these "wait and sees" responded, in addition to some others whose first applications had been declined and who had subsequently been counseled by the project director. In all, 107 participants were selected from 147 applicants, and the four classes met the criteria for the make-up of classes described earlier. The selection subcommittee of the project advisory team arranged their recommendations in rank order but gave the project director the prerogative of selecting some ranked lower (but "passing") to provide for individual class balance and distribution.

Retreat and Class Sessions. Four classes were scheduled over a fifteen-month period. Each class included a two-day retreat and eight weekly one-day class sessions. In general, three major ideas or skills were emphasized. The earlier period emphasized intra- and intergroup interaction and communication. The emphasis was then shifted to an understanding of the organization and operations of a university. The skills and understandings developed during these stages were then applied to issues in higher education and specific problems and needs of The University of Akron as an urban institution. The two statements on urban mission and goals and purposes, coupled with selected readings, provided the basis for the retreat and the class sessions.

The format of the retreat and class sessions included presentations, discussions, demonstrations, simulations, role playing, and other participative exercises. The objective of the three-stage approach was to develop diagnostic skills as well as leadership and team-building skills that could be applied to areas of need identified through the use of these diagnostic skills.

An external consultant, David DeShon, was appointed to assist in the development of the exercises and to serve as a cotrainer with the project director. Participants were selected to serve as training assistants in classes II, III, and IV. Participants were also encouraged to develop exercises consistent with the objectives of the program in their own area of expertise and to provide leadership for these exercises.

Each retreat took place off campus with bus transportation provided for the class members and trainers. Although the weekly sessions were held on campus, they took place in a "penthouse" with a view of the movement between the city and the campus that symbolized the spirit of the program. Approximately seventy-five different exercises were developed by the trainers for the classes, including handouts and selected reading assignments. A trainer's guide was developed for each exercise and made available to participants in case they wished to use the exercise in other situations. The following premises were the basis of the training program:

1. Leadership is often erroneously equated with top management positions. Actually, many degrees and types of leadership need to be exercised at all levels. Further, good management alone is not necessarily good leadership.

2. Team leadership training requires a sound grounding in concepts *and* practice. Therefore, emphasis was placed on learning through involvement, with subtle and consistent instruction in leadership principles.

3. Interpersonal and communication skills are basic and critical to good leadership, particularly team leadership. Further, the ability to listen is basic to sound interpersonal and communication skills.

4. Although the basic principles of leadership are essentially constant irrespective of the organization, application of these principles frequently takes on a unique character when applied to the university setting.

The design of the retreats and class sessions anticipated the recommendations of Trist (1977) and Kouzes and Mico (1979) for the creation of collaborative processes to unify the otherwise separate domains of policy, management, and service indigenous to university structures. That is, a "temporary domain" was "created to enhance cooperation and joint endeavor." This domain was guided by the principles of inquiry and experimentation; was characterized by an informal structure, that is, few levels of authority, low division of labor, and multiple representation by each domain; used creative problem-solving techniques; encouraged constructive confrontation, collaboration, and critique; and used creativity and innovation as partial measures of success.

Task Forces. Time was provided during each session for the class to break into groups and practice their team leadership concepts as they identified task force activities to pursue following the formal class sessions. At the completion of each of the four classes, these recommendations were presented to the president of the university for his approval. Eighteen task forces were formed over the two-year period to pursue the following goals:

- Develop a better understanding among the faculty and staff of the university mission and goals
- Improve internal communication
- Review the university's performance evaluation and reward system

- Develop greater interaction with the northeastern Ohio region
- Explore the feasibility of developing an active faculty club
- Provide more information to a broader spectrum of the campus concerning the university's service units
- Encourage interdisciplinary activities on campus
- Integrate experiential learning into the university curriculum
- Extend the team leadership program beyond its two-year grant period
- Develop new approaches to lifelong education
- Enhance the intellectual climate at the university
- Form an exchange network between the university and public and private area high schools
- Explore the use of retirees as resource persons on campus
- Investigate risk management implications in university administration
- Improve classroom teaching
- Establish a referral and support system for handicapped students
- Provide a process for deans and department heads to improve their management skills
- Explore the possibilities of designing a team leadership training program for students.

After the task forces were organized and underway, the project staff worked closely with the task force chairmen to help integrate the activities of the task forces that overlapped ongoing university activities. Other unduplicated activities of the task forces continued on their own, and still others atrophied and faded away. To date, the following results can be identified with the activities of the task forces:

- The revision and updating of The University of Akron's statement of urban mission and goals
- The establishment of an internal campus newsletter
- The establishment of a study of the university's performance evaluation and reward system
- The acquisition of a building and the development of a strong university club involving faculty, alumni, and friends of the university
- A number of activities extending the team leadership program into the campus mainstream
- The establishment of the "school-university network" composed of faculty from a variety of colleges and representatives of area high schools

- An inventory and directory of referral and support services for handicapped students on campus
- A miniteam leadership workshop for department heads
- A proposal for extending the team leadership program to include students and community members (subsequently funded by the W. K. Kellogg Foundation).

Internships. The program provided for eight interns to be selected from the participants to spend up to 50 percent of their time for twelve months in administrative or academic departments other than their own. More intern applicants would have been possible if policies concerning release time had been more flexible, if the increasing enrollment demands had not created heavier teaching loads for most of the faculty, and if appropriate replacements had been available.

The eight interns were to work on specific problems that involved team building and that supported the university's urban mission. The projects were to be defined cooperatively by the intern, the project director, the intern's home department, and the department in which he or she would be doing the internship. In all cases, faculty and administrators would become familiar with other aspects and operations of the university so that teams cutting across different units of the university would be established. The selection of interns was made by a subcommittee of the program advisory group based on the applicant's qualifications, competencies, and proposed program; the areas of university organization development to be emphasized; and the potential of the internship for furthering team leadership development. Eight internships were awarded for the following projects:

- Planning and training in the team leadership development program
- Identification of available management information data on campus
- Encouraging instructional innovation in modern languages and establishing cooperative programs with area schools
- Exploring the potential for greater growth in continuing education for professionals
- Investigating the feasibility of a combined engineering and management postbaccalaureate professional degree
- Gaining experience in the development function and relating it to the needs of the university's performing arts hall
- Creating a council of agencies engaged in educational activities in the Akron area
- Stimulating off-campus teaching activities.

Miniteam Leadership Workshops and Team Leadership Break-fast Forums. As participants carried the information concerning the program back to their departments and colleges, the Office of Team Leadership Development began to receive requests for miniteam leadership programs. The original program design recognized the possibility that participants in the classes might develop less extensive programs for their own departments or units, thus reinforcing the learnings of the program and promoting an environment conducive to continuing growth in leadership. In addition to the 107 persons participating in the main classes of the team leadership program, approximately 200 others were participants in the miniteam leadership programs. Experience with these programs revealed that the same learnings were equally applicable and of interest to nonprofessional staff, and in fact, worked well when faculty, administration, and clerical staff from the same department were included in the same workshops. For each of the miniteam leadership workshops, a member of the Office of Team Leadership Development project staff met with a designated group from the department that had requested the workshop and designed the program in cooperation with these representatives. The department itself handled all logistics and costs related to the team leadership workshops.

To increase the understanding of the relationships of issues in higher education to our everyday campus activities, to help continue the cohesiveness of the classes, and to develop new cohesiveness among participants from different classes, a series of team leadership breakfast forums was initiated. Resource persons active in areas related to higher education issues and generally well known at the national level were brought to campus, often in cooperation with other campus groups, to share their perspectives of the challenges in higher education with the team leadership class members and related groups such as the project advisory group, the commission on institutional planning and development, and the president's staff. Attendance at these forums has been consistently high — 70 to 120 — since their inception.

Evaluation. Two concurrent evaluations of the program were conducted. The first, a formative one, assessed the effectiveness of each aspect of the program as it was conducted, thus enabling the trainers to modify and improve subsequent classes. The formative evaluation included group growth inventories, self-appraisal, assessment by each class of the activities planned for them, and suggestions for improving activities for future classes. In addition, class members were asked to supply anecdotal notes concerning places and ways in which participants used the learning from the team leadership program, the participants' perceptions of the goals of the program, and the extent to which these goals were achieved.

The second evaluation approach, a summative one, was conducted by external consultants in team-leadership development and organizational change and was designed to give an objective view of the effectiveness of the program. This evaluation was conducted primarily by questionnaires and interviews. An in-house component of the summative evaluation measured the impact of the Kellogg program by using a pre- and post-campus survey covering (1) the motivation and organizational climates, (2) descriptions of the behaviors of leaders (ideal), and (3) a measure of interdependence in communication between university organizational units.

While noting that the full effects of the program may not yet have been felt, the external evaluators did summarize some preliminary findings:

1. The participants, in general, experienced increased personal development and knowledge of leadership and management issues.
2. Communications among participants increased.
3. There was a slightly increased capability to coordinate university activities in programs across departmental lines.
4. Task force projects had not yet made substantial contributions to university functioning as of the date of the evaluation. Further, these projects were seen by many as addressing unmanageable or unimportant problems.
5. Intern projects were seen by many as duplicative of regular university job assignments although the full effects of the projects could not yet be reported as of the time of the evaluation (Lippitt and Aurelio, 1976).

Although it is difficult to establish any causal relationship between the team leadership program and the results of the pre- and post-campus survey, there were some significant differences between participants and nonparticipants in feelings of acceptance by the campus and community and understanding of leadership behavior.

Epilogue

Today, four years after the beginning of the program and two years after its completion, 14 of the 107 participants have left the university for employment elsewhere. Several of them did not continue in higher education. Of these 14 participants, 4 had broadened their university, professional, or community involvement prior to their departure. Fifteen participants had received promotions or job changes within the university indicating a promotion, other than academic rank advancement, and 22 had noticeably increased their involvement in university, professional, or community activities.

Placing the program in a larger perspective, it may be interesting to share some thoughts concerning what we would change if we were to do it again. We knew that organizational development had advanced to the point that a full catalog of procedures existed to help an organization prepare for and deal with change. We also knew that the few colleges and universities employing these procedures were generally experiencing limited and short-range success. The reasons were that most campus programs dealing with change limited themselves to only one area, such as interpersonal, group, organizational, or mission/task; most published techniques did not address themselves directly to the distinctive organizational problems/needs of colleges and universities; and the techniques used dealt primarily with "lower-order change," that is, change in outcomes but not necessarily in the system.

In response to our perception of these problems, we included the following strategies in our program: First, we developed a team leadership program across three major dimensions of understanding: (1) interpersonal, intergroup, and intragroup; (2) university organizations; and (3) issues in higher education and their applicability to our own university. Our intention was to move the participant from individual awareness through group understanding into a more complete sense of the total organization, its dynamic, and the interrelations of individual, groups, and organization. From here, we moved on to the national scene as it affected higher education in general and our own university and its mission in particular. In brief, we tried to develop a transcending awareness of the individual, group, organization, and national scene. A melding of these three thrusts into one program made this particular program unique to the best of our knowledge. This approach helped us maintain the broader view of systems improvement.

Second, we recast the techniques for team leadership training into the university context and developed new exercises within this context when none were known to exist. This allowed us to deal with the distinct needs of an urban university. Third, recognizing that our program by itself was a lower-order change effort, we developed it as an integral part of a total network of change, providing the potential for changing both outcomes and processes.

Typically, programs of this type assume that once participants have learned new concepts and have made these new concepts a part of their way of thinking, they will naturally carry these concepts into practice and build on them. Unfortunately, this is not a valid assumption (for example, see Argyris, 1976). Therefore, we built into the team leadership development program expectations of application of the concepts learned, including class exercises, task forces, and internships.

So much for the perspective, the setting, our assumptions, and our expectations. Within this perspective, what happened? What would we change? What would we keep the same? Our first reflection concerns our approach to moving the program to the level of higher-order change. The major change we would make here would be one of timing. Rather than establishing the team leadership program first and then identifying the balance of the network, we would start with the commission on institutional planning and development. This body—or a subcommittee—would also have served as the program advisory group. From here, the team leadership program would follow essentially the same design with the following exceptions: First, members of the commission on institutional planning and development plus representatives of the commission's primary source areas would constitute the first of five classes, with the four remaining classes following the participant distribution procedure used in the original program. Second, the issues dealt with by the task forces and internships would be developed in close cooperation with the commission. However, even without the wisdom of hindsight, we were able slowly to move the team leadership program into the above relationship. Further, the commission membership included a good representation of Kellogg participants.

Our second reflection relates to the efficacy of building expectations of an application of the concepts learned into the program. Although, as reported above, the program was designed to achieve this expectation, we were not as successful as we might have been. The heavy commitment of time and energy to the design, conduct, and the evaluation of the retreat and class phase for this program, as contrasted with the "autonomy-approaching laissez faire" approach to monitoring task forces and internships belied our exclamations of equal emphasis. Again, using the wisdom of hindsight, we would take the attitude and action that the primary thrusts of the program were the activities of the task forces and the internships. All other activities (for example, retreats and classes) would be preparation for and supportive of these primary thrusts. The relationship with the commission proposed above would reinforce this attitude.

Our third and last reflection is general, evaluative, and subjective. As tempted as we might be to say that the program would have profited if we had provided more instruction in one area rather than another, the truth probably is that the results would be the same. We diagnosed the needs of our university and constructed a program accordingly. Time precluded the inclusion of everything we would like to have covered. However, each class provided its own shifts of emphases and its own reservoir of talent and insight. The result was a broad, standardized curriculum that each class tailored to its own needs.

Was the program successful? We do not know for certain and probably never will. We have seen positive changes on The University of Akron campus for which we are willing to take credit, but we cross our fingers when we do. We know that the program has touched over 300 of our faculty and staff through classes, miniteam leadership programs, and breakfast forums. We know that early changes are happening as a result of internships and task force activities. An esprit de corps continues among the participants even now. Others, nonparticipants, are drawn into the use of the new vocabulary of age-old concepts. We continue to receive requests for more team leadership classes from those who were unable or unwilling to take part in the first round of classes. And we sense a real and positive movement on the campus—a sense of direction and a sense of unity. Forces are in motion; activities are in process. We do not know if the program has worked, but we do feel that it is working.

References

Argyris, C. *Increasing Leadership Effectiveness*. New York: Wiley, 1976.

Balderston, F. E. *Managing Today's University*. San Francisco: Jossey-Bass, 1974.

Buchtel, F. S., and Guzzetta, D. J. "The W. K. Kellogg Foundation Program for the Development of Team Leadership at The University of Akron." In *Proceedings*, Academic Administrative Workshops, 9th Annual Conference. Chicago: American Institute for Decision Sciences, 1977.

Buchtel, F. S. "Integrating Planning and Institutional Research in Medium-Size Universities." In P. Jedamus and M. Peterson (Eds.), *Improving Academic Management: A Handbook of Planning and Institutional Research*. San Francisco: Jossey-Bass, 1980.

Guzzetta, D. J. "Facing a Changing Future with a Sense of Community." In *Proceedings*, 18th Annual Conference, American Association of State Colleges and Universities, Washington, D.C., 1978.

Kouzes, J. M., and Mico, P. R. "Domain Theory: An Introduction to Organizational Behavior in Human Service Organizations." *Journal of Applied Behavioral Science*, 1979, *15*, (4), 449–469.

Lippitt, G., and Aurelio, J. "Evaluation Report," *W. K. Kellogg Foundation Program for the Development of Team Leadership at an Urban University*. Washington, D.C.: Project Associates, 1976.

Lippitt, G. *Organizational Renewal*. New York: Appleton-Century-Crofts, 1969.

Michael, D. N. *On Learning to Plan—and Planning to Learn: The Social Psychology of Changing Toward Future-Responsive Societal Learning*. San Francisco: Jossey-Bass, 1973.

Ohio Board of Regents. *Planning/Universities.* Columbus, Ohio: Ohio Board of Regents, 1973.

Ozbekhan, H. "Toward a General Theory of Planning." In B. Jantsch (Ed.), *Perspectives of Planning.* Paris: Organization for Economic Cooperation and Development, 1969.

Sayles, L. R. "Matrix Management: The Structure with a Future." In *Organizational Dynamics.* New York: American Management Association, 1976.

Trist, E. "Collaboration in Work Settings: A Personal Perspective." *Journal of Applied Behavioral Science,* 1977, *13* (3), 268-278.

Foster S. Buchtel, assistant to the president of The University of Akron, has primary responsibility for program change and development; policy and issue analysis; and institutional research. He served as project director of Team Leadership at an Urban University and is currently project director for Development of a Model Network of University/Community Team Leadership.

Problems will arise in a systematic approach to planned change, but the potential is great and the risks less than the other major options available to college and university administrators at the present time.

Case Study: The Furman Experience

Philip C. Winstead

In a complex organization, change is seldom easy whether it is planned or brought about by impulse. Yet, in recent years, the need for change in institutions of higher education has become more acute. During the past decade and a half, the administration and faculty at Furman University have been keenly aware that the college needed to respond to the forces of change in order to retain its reputation for academic excellence as well as to respond to new areas of service. Therefore, in 1971, with grants from the Ford Foundation and the Exxon Education Foundation, Furman initiated a comprehensive effort to develop a management planning model that would serve not only its needs but also the needs of similar institutions. The model developed is a decentralized, participative approach to institutional governance that stresses decision making based on use of appropriate research and allocation of resources based on management by objectives. The initial effort in the management planning program was directed toward the administrative operation of the university. Only after the success of the program was demonstrated in this area was it tested in the planning and management of the academic program.

G. Hipps (Ed.). *New Directions for Institutional Research: Effective Planned Change Strategies*, no. 33. San Francisco: Jossey-Bass, March 1982.

Furman University

Furman University is a Baptist, coeducational, liberal arts college located in Greenville, South Carolina. Founded in 1826, it currently has an undergraduate student body of approximately 2,400 and a faculty of 155. Furman, although steeped in tradition, is not new to innovation and change. Within the past twenty years Furman has moved from a congested location in downtown Greenville to a spacious campus on the outskirts of town. The curriculum has been reorganized to provide for independent study, foreign study, off-campus internships and research, and interdisciplinary courses. In addition to the undergraduate curriculum, Furman maintains small graduate programs in education, chemistry, and business administration. The university has a progressive administration, an excellent faculty, a student body with academic qualifications above the average, and a belief that all members of the academic community should participate appropriately in planning and decision making.

Five Basic Decisions

At the time Furman made the decision to pursue the program in systematic planning, those involved were aware that a piecemeal approach to something as complex as this could very well do more harm than good. Consequently, several basic decisions were made at the outset:

1. It was decided to institute a systems approach to change. It was recognized that different parts of the institution affect each other, and that change in one part creates change in another.

2. Every attempt would be made to minimize surprise. Any significant change would be difficult if those affected by the changes were not aware of them before the changes were introduced.

3. Several "go" and "no-go" decision points would be built into the schedule. This type of flexibility would be necessary to gain the initial support of those involved.

4. Furman would provide the support needed to ensure that the program had a fair chance to succeed.

5. All involved would adhere to a "golden rule of common sense and value." Furman would not change just for the sake of change. It would not move any further or faster than the

participants felt desirable, and thorough evaluation would take place as part of every phase of the program.

Twelve Critical Factors

Early in the development stage, twelve factors were identified that the university leadership believed were critical to effective institutional planning:

1. Make sure there is general agreement regarding management style, organizational relationships, and information requirements before engaging in any type of organized, systematic planning.
2. Clarify basic policies and establish general guidelines before getting too deeply involved in substantive planning.
3. Take appropriate steps to avoid rumors and to gain acceptance and support for the planning efforts.
4. Create a planning environment and provide a practical planning process before asking people to engage in planning activities.
5. Make sure the planning process is designed to meet the needs and requirements of the institution, not just a copy of someone else's process. Of course, one should not reinvent the wheel but neither should one blindly accept a process developed by others.
6. Provide enough flexibility to meet changing conditions and enough adaptability to be able to cope with all of the types of planning that need to be done.
7. Get and keep in focus adequate decision-making information at the times and places where it is needed.
8. Be sure that the planning process makes it possible to revise agreement as well as to reach agreement.
9. Be sure to identify and monitor all important developments that will have a major impact on future performance or results.
10. Continually identify and evaluate the institution's capabilities and opportunities as well as the strengths and weaknesses.
11. Keep the planning process simple and minimize paper work.
12. Provide staff support for planning. Do not let staff people do the planning but conserve the time of key people in the institution as much as possible.

The Furman Planning Program

To initiate and steer the program, a committee on institutional planning was created and charged with the overall direction of the program. The committee, chaired by the president, included the four vice-presidents, two deans, the business manager, the director of communications, heads of two academic and administrative committees, eight faculty members, two students, a trustee, and a member of the alumni association.

At the same time, an external group, a management task force, was appointed by the university's advisory council and charged with the responsibility of providing advice to the effort. The members of the advisory council are business and professional leaders throughout the country who work closely with Furman's administration in matters in which their experience can be valuable.

The original project was designed to consist of three phases. During phase I, the committee on institutional planning continued the discussion concerning management and planning that had been initiated several months earlier with Planning Dynamics, Inc. (PDI), a management consultant firm, which had had successful experience with various nonprofit organizations by using an approach to planning that enhances participation and provides flexibility. Furman's committee on institutional planning reaffirmed the belief that the work of PDI could form the nucleus of the planning and management model envisioned for use at Furman. At the same time, the committee was conducting a preliminary analysis of the institution in terms of readiness for the program and orienting key participants to the project to make sure that the nature, scope, and purpose were clearly understood. The orientation consisted of in-depth discussions with administrators, faculty, students and staff. The decision to move into phase II was made only after careful consideration by this committee. This was one of the "go," "no-go" points mentioned earlier.

Phase II was the design of a hypothetical management planning model for Furman that met the agreed upon specifications. Furman used consultants from PDI while a prototype planning system was developed. A workshop was held for key administrators and faculty to demonstrate the applicability of the tentative model. The committee on institutional planning again decided whether or not to continue with the project.

The decision at the end of phase II was favorable for moving into phase III, the full development and implementation stage. At this time, an office of institutional planning and research was created, and a person was hired to fill the staff position of planning specialist or coordinator of institutional planning and research. Nine key elements provide the essence of the program:

Goal Clarification. Furman participated in an institutional goals study using the Delphi technique as a means to investigate how various constituents perceived the goals of the institution as well as what they thought the goals should be. The instrument used in the study was a preliminary version of the Institutional Goals Inventory (IGI) developed by the Educational Testing Service. The results of this study provided the background for development of goals, both for the university as a whole and for each of the organizational units within the institution.

Management by Objectives. With goals as a foundation, each organizational unit derived measurable objectives from the goals and tested a management-by-objectives approach to administration. A workshop was held in which selected budget unit heads participated in a series of activities designed to help them analyze their goals, specify measurable objectives, and reach agreement with members of their staff in the assignment of responsibilities.

The management-by-objectives technique used at Furman requires that objectives for a given organizational unit be derived by members of that unit and reviewed by appropriate higher echelons of the organization. At this point, the individual objectives are checked for consistency with the university objectives before they are authorized. Responsibility for each objective is then assigned to the appropriate person, and the available resources are made known to him. Review sessions involving each employee and his supervisor are held periodically. At the end of the fiscal year, the actual results are jointly reviewed against the agreed upon goals and objectives. It is at this point that the evaluation influences the reward system. The strength of the process is in the focus on results, the provisions for feedback, and the commitment arising from participant involvement in this process.

Strengths, Weaknesses, Opportunities, Threats (SWOTs Analysis). It was recognized very early that the program of management by objectives had to deal with the problem of limited resources. An institution never has enough resources to do everything that it wants to do and everything that can be justified. Therefore, management is defined as the ability of the institution to create, conserve, and use its resources to accomplish the things that are most important. Therefore, before an objective is authorized, it is weighed against criteria such as value, feasibility, flexibility, and measurability.

In order to make these judgments, each functional unit does a

SWOTs analysis in the form of an annual report. SWOTs, discussed in Chapter Two, is an acronym for a self-appraisal in which each organizational unit examines the Strengths, Weaknesses, Opportunities, and Threats within that unit. Next, the SWOTs of each individual unit are consolidated into a university-wide analysis. The SWOTs analysis thus provides a framework, along with institutional goals and available resources, for establishing priorities among the proposed objectives. As a result, objectives can be authorized that maximize strengths, minimize weaknesses, capitalize on opportunities, or eliminate or minimize threats of the individual units as well as the university as a whole.

Planning Book. A planning book system serves as the chief organizing vehicle for the entire process. It is the way in which purpose, goals, objectives, management by objectives, basic data, and other elements of systematic planning are integrated into the university's ongoing administrative processes. The planning book is a loose-leaf notebook with color-coded pages, which can be updated individually. The contents are organized by the data categories that are needed to provide information for decision making.

All the pertinent information is not contained in one planning book. If it were, the book would be unmanageable and would defeat the purpose of the system. Information is included on a need-to-know basis. Consequently, the contents differ in part for each individual book holder depending on his area of responsibility. The material that is applicable to the university as a whole is found in all planning books, but each book differs according to the operations and needs of the various organization units.

Policies and Procedures System. Early in the program it was found that any systematic approach to management planning cannot function effectively if appropriate and clearly stated policies and procedures are not in existence for those involved in planning and decision making. Policies give consistency to planning and decision making but still allow different decisions on different sets of facts. Each individual responsible for a department, function, or activity is responsible for seeing that appropriate policies, procedures, and guidelines are formulated, distributed, revised, and maintained. No individual, however, issues policies and procedures that conflict with those issued by a higher authority.

In order to initiate the policies and procedures system, five special task forces were appointed to recommend university-wide policies in the areas of governance, organizational relationships, growth, institutional identity, and policies. The faculty status committee was asked to revise the faculty handbook consistent with the new format, and the vice-president for business affairs was asked to oversee the conversion of the business office procedures manual to the new system. As with the planning book, all policies and procedures are maintained in loose-leaf binders of color-coded pages with specific file numbers. Distribution is on a need-to-know basis.

Computer-Based Information Systems. At the time Furman decided to plan for planning, a computer-based generalized information retrieval system and a computerized general ledger system, which could be keyed to both a line-item budget and a program budget, already existed. Believing that a computer-based simulation model was also important to the planning process, members of the planning staff determined that two were applicable to the needs at Furman: (1) the original HELP version of HELP/PLANTRAN to simulate revenue and resource allocation functions and (2) the NCHEMS/RRPM 1.6 model to answer questions concerning the effects of curriculum changes, decreases in students in various major fields, and the effects of these changes on all the academic departments. The goal was always to provide the decision maker with current, comprehensive information at the times and places where the decisions and plans were being made.

Institutional Research. Institutional research activities were conducted continuously to address special problems and to provide administrators and faculty with alternatives for decision making. Two types of research documents are used for distribution: (1) a planning report series dealing with topics of general interest and with university-wide applicability, and (2) a planning memo series responding to specific requests by administrators or faculty members. All institutional research is action oriented. Examples of the topics are reports on the success of academic prediction at Furman, student attrition rates, summer session enrollment patterns, classroom use, the effect of the academic probation rule on undergraduate students, the postgraduation plans for Furman graduates, departmental grade distribution, and characteristics of freshmen.

Priorities Task Force. A priorities task force was created as a subcommittee of the committee on institutional planning to address the persistent problem of how to decide among worthwhile activities across major units of the university. The task force was charged with examining all aspects of Furman's operations and making recommendations to the president regarding the expenditures that make the greatest contribution toward achieving Furman's primary goals and appropriate ways of balancing expenditures with income.

Advice and Training. The advisory and training activities were interspersed continuously through the planning process. For example in addition to providing general guidance, the committee on institutional planning provided the means by which the work in management planning was assimilated into the regular operating procedures of the university, and the management task force of the advisory council produced specific reports suggesting ways of improving institutional effectiveness and efficiency and was helpful in assessing the environment and developing reliable assumptions for planning purposes. Also, workshops were held for all of the administrators at the university to discuss the conceptual base for the project and the implementation techniques. The president continued his practice of holding administrative council retreats each summer to discuss the major issues facing the university and to finalize the university-wide SWOTs analysis.

Faculty Development in Academic Planning

When the leadership of the university was satisfied that a systematic planning process was operating in the administrative area with sufficient success to warrant moving it into the academic area, Furman submitted a proposal to the W. K. Kellogg Foundation for a program entitled "Faculty Development in Academic Planning: An Approach to Institutional Self-Renewal." This three-year program supported by Kellogg (1975–1978) became phase IV in the planned change program at Furman. Again, a steering committee was appointed. However, this time the committee, although involving administrators as well as faculty, was a faculty committee and was elected by the usual procedure for electing faculty committees. This process ensured faculty ownership of the program. This program trained faculty members in systematic planning techniques and allowed them to revise courses, develop new courses, or try new instructional strategies.

The Kellogg-sponsored project was designed to enhance the learning experiences of students by improving the ability of the faculty to plan appropriate courses and programs and to adopt new instructional techniques as a part of their teaching methodology. The primary objectives of the faculty development project were as follows:

- To develop and implement an ongoing institutional self-renewal program for effective faculty development and academic planning
- To involve more faculty including release time for academic renewal activities.

- To make faculty more aware of innovative and successful academic programs, relating to Furman's interests, in other colleges and universities
- To increase the exposure of faculty to specialists in academic planning and to leading professionals in the various academic disciplines
- To update and upgrade the expertise of faculty in emerging teaching methodologies and techniques
- To expand research opportunities and support services to the level required to ensure the professional and intellectual growth of the faculty
- To improve morale and promote intellectual exchange among the faculty, both within departments and between departments and divisions
- To develop new administrative mechanisms better suited to accommodate interdisciplinary programs.

Planning Activities. The Kellogg project supported two types of planning activities—individual activities and departmental, divisional, or institutional activities. Additionally, there was a series of colloquia, designed to acquaint faculty with some recent trends and issues in higher education, and a series of planning orientation sessions to assist faculty in becoming more proficient in skills involved in planning. Each faculty member who wished to do so submitted a proposal to the steering committee (see Figure 1). Final selection of projects was made by the committee on the basis of this information. Each faculty member was asked to evaluate his project by submitting an evaluation report. One of the major links between this project and the institutional management program was the requirement that each proposal state the relationship between the proposed activities and the SWOTs analysis of a department, a division, or the university.

The funding level for individual projects was $400 to $700, and the money could be spent on travel, consultants, materials, and so forth—as long as it was spent for academic planning as opposed to program implementation. Departmental, divisional, and institutional planning activities, although proposed and carried out by a single faculty member, were supposed to concern the work of an entire department, division, or the entire college. The amount allocated for these activities ranged from $1,000 to $1,200. The project paid for a replacement for one course for each faculty member directing a departmental, divisional, or institutional planning project.

Fifty-nine faculty members (41 percent of the full-time faculty)

Figure 1. Kellogg Planning Project Proposal
Departmental, Divisional, or Institutional Activity

ORIGINATOR:

DISTRIBUTION: Kellogg Steering Committee

PROJECT TITLE:

	THIS	REPLACES
FILE :		
DATE :		
PAGE :	1 of 2	

A. DESCRIPTION OF THE PLANNING PROJECT

B. OBJECTIVES OF THE PLANNING PROJECT

C. WAYS IN WHICH PROPOSED PROJECT RELATES TO A STRENGTH, WEAKNESS, OPPORTUNITY, OR THREAT (SWOTS ANALYSIS) OF A DEPARTMENT, A DIVISION, OR OF THE UNIVERSITY

D. SCHEDULE: (BEGINNING AND FNDING DATES)

ORIGINATOR:

DISTRIBUTION:

PROJECT TITLE:

	THIS	REPLACES
FILE :		
DATE :		
PAGE :	2 of 2	

E. BUDGET:

   1. STAFF TRAVEL (INCLUDE PER DIEM)

   2. CONSULTANTS (INCLUDE TRAVEL AND PER DIEM)

   3. TOTAL BUDGET

F. SUPPORT SERVICES NEEDED (ESTIMATE COST OF EACH SERVICE)

   1. TELEPHONING

   2. SUPPLIES

   3. DUPLICATION

   4. OTHER

   5. TOTAL

G. RESPONSIBILITY: (INDICATE WHO WILL COORDINATE THE PROJECT AND THE DATES OF THE RELEASED TIME REQUESTED)

*Attach support letter from departmental chairman if this is a departmental project; from the chairman of each department in a division for a divisional project, or from the Dean for an institutional project.

completed planning projects under the auspices of the Kellogg grant. Their planning involved developing or revising courses, trying new instructional modes, and studying certain topics of interest to the university. Among the new courses developed were an interdisciplinary course in art, drama, and music; developmental biology; teaching the gifted and talented student; teaching English to speakers of other languages; a new general education course in philosophy; politics and morality; limits to growth (sciology); and artificial intelligence (computer science). Some new programs were an alumni feedback program in economics and business administration; mainstreaming (special education); learning resources laboratories in mathematics and biology; comparative literature; self-taught, self-paced instruction in exotic languages; a Washington term project; and bibliographic instruction in the use of the library. New instructional techniques included the use of the Personalized System of Instruction (Keller Plan), a modular organization of the precalculus course, a team-taught methods course (education), computer assisted instruction, and strategies for teaching class piano.

Special Colloquia and Planning Orientations. For each of the three years of the program, two to four special colloquia were planned according to a predetermined theme for the year, with the intent of presenting new thoughts and academic activities to the Furman faculty. These activities were intended to stimulate thought and generate new ideas for possible new programmatic efforts on campus. The theme for the first year, "The Purpose and Scope of a Liberal Arts College," was supported by four special colloquia conducted by off-campus scholars and practitioners on the subjects, "The Future of the Liberal Arts College," "Role of Policy Study in a Liberal Arts College," "Evaluating Teaching and Teacher Effectiveness," and "General Education— Philosophy, Requirements, and Recent Issues and Trends." The second and third year themes were "Alternative Instructional Strategies" and "The Role of Values in Higher Education."

The planning orientation phase of the program was designed to increase the awareness of the faculty of the value and necessity of systematic planning. The intent was to provide instruction in the planning process being tested, to relate general planning principles to academic planning, to share with the Furman faculty knowledge gained by participants in the project, and to bring to campus outside speakers and consultants to advise different faculty groups on substantive issues. Four to six planning orientations were held in each of the three years of the project. They included sessions on the nature of faculty development in academic planning, the need for faculty renewal, basic planning principles, team building and leadership training, and approaches to faculty evaluation.

Evaluation

Administrative Program. The evaluation of the management planning program consisted of three activities: (1) the primary consultant for the project prepared a written critique of the program; (2) a team of nationally known educators visited the campus, examined the program, and prepared a written report on the degree to which the objectives of the project were met; (3) the office of institutional planning and research administered a survey to those on campus who were involved in the project to ascertain their attitudes and opinions concerning the planning program and its impact on the university.

The consultant complimented the administration's understanding and acceptance of decentralized, participative managerial style and the development of an effective planning prototype to meet the unique needs of the university. The visiting team observed that the management information system had proved helpful in policy analysis, in operational activities, and in a furtherance of openness and discussion at Furman. They analyzed the structural organization for carrying out the planning process as "functioning well," including extensive direction, planning coordination, and the committee on institutional planning; and they complimented the planning book as being practical and helpful.

The opinion survey, administered to ninety persons who held or had held the planning book, revealed general support for the management planning program including support for management by objectives. The planning book was seen as one of the strongest features of the program. The institutional research function was also viewed favorably.

Among the criticisms from the three evaluations were the following: (1) The planning data dealing with projections should be more dynamically quantified so that deviations can be more easily detected, (2) paperwork should be reduced, (3) feedback linkages should be improved, and (4) the annual budget should be developed around agreed upon objectives and plans. The results of the three evaluations warranted the conclusion that overall progress in the project had been substantial.

Faculty Program. The evaluation design for the faculty development in academic planning program also consisted of three activities. The first was the administering of two surveys to everyone on campus holding faculty rank. The first questionnaire was designed "to determine certain basic knowledge, understandings, feelings, and attitudes about the project" in order to gauge the initial opinions concerning the project and the levels of concern among the faculty about faculty development in academic planning. Near the end of the project, a second survey was administered to measure possible changes in behavior and concepts.

The second evaluation activity was the use of an external team who visited the campus throughout the grant period to provide independent formative and summative evaluations. The team interviewed faculty and staff involved in Kellogg-related activities, reviewed project-related materials, made suggestions and raised questions as a formative evaluation near the mid-point of the project, and near the end of the project assessed progress toward the accomplishment of the program objectives was a summative evaluation.

The third evaluation activity was the subjective assessment by the project codirectors and the Kellogg project steering committee. As a part of his final planning activity report, the project director of each individual, departmental, divisional, and institutional level planning activity evaluated his project.

The three evaluations for the faculty development program were generally positive. The faculty surveys showed the following: (1) Agreement that the basic premises on which the program was based had not changed significantly between the presurvey evaluation and the post survey; (2) the opinion of the faculty about the characteristics of Furman University, and the role of the faculty in decision making areas had not changed; (3) the sections evaluating overall effectiveness and the degree to which objectives of the project had been met were answered by the faculty with responses that showed satisfaction with the way the project had been conducted, the usefulness of the techniques and procedures, and the impact of the program on individuals and on the university.

For the external evaluation team, an assessment of the extent to which project objectives were accomplished was the key issue. The team lauded the project on the relevance of the objectives to the needs of the university and of higher education generally. They pointed out that accomplishment of some of the objectives was still somewhat problematic. They raised questions about the degree to which faculty expertise in academic planning had increased and about the extent to which students had been involved in academic planning. The evaluators concluded, however, that when arraying and examining the apparent accumulative effects of the project's objectives, ". . . what is most evident is that the project has made a strong contribution to the institutional renewal and faculty development at Furman University."

Evaluations of the fifty-nine planning activities were mixed. Many of the activities were highly successful and demonstrated indentifiable behavioral changes among faculty as well as a great impact upon students in the classroom. Planning activities dealing with individualized and self-paced instruction fell into this category. Planning activities noted for their potential were those concerning general education requirements, increased use of technology, values in the curriculum, and interdisciplinary courses. Some planning activities were well done, but their potential impact was limited. Others were marginal in value at best. The final reports did reveal a genuine desire in most cases to test the management planning procedures fairly and in all cases a desire of the faculty member to improve Furman's educational program in some tangible way.

Looking Back

It is natural in programs like the one at Furman to reflect on what might have been done differently to increase the impact of the projects or on what was done that enhanced the success of the projects. Concerning the initial management planning project, as might be expected, there was initial resistance among some persons to any type of change. The university, however, relied on what it believed to be a reasonable and open approach to change, and consequently, there was not any organized opposition to the management planning program or to the management-by-objectives approach. Rather, the resistance to change took the form of conceptual disagreements and debate regarding the success, failure, or value of various aspects of the program. A key element was the strategy of a series of workshops to discuss the need for the program, the conceptual base for the management planning/management-by-objectives projects, and the various techniques for program implementation. These sessions, which were designed to inform rather than indoctrinate, emphasized the building and maintaining of the support necessary for success.

A second important element was the phasing of the project and the inclusion of the two "go" or "no-go" decision points in the implementation strategy. The realization by the on-campus participants that formative evaluation was taking place and that the program would be aborted or altered if the evaluations were not positive gave a great deal of credibility to the program. A third decision that proved to be a distinct asset to the success of the program was the use of unbiased, well-respected off-campus persons to serve as the primary evaluators of the program. This process contributed significantly to the openness with which the project was pursued. Finally, the decision by the president to support the project actively and to give visible and continuous leadership to it was a major key to its success. He initiated the planning for a systematic management planning program and assumed a leadership role in the program by chairing the committee on institutional planning, adhering to the management-by-objectives procedures and schedules adopted, following the systematic planning procedures, and seeing that the administrator evaluations resulting from the project did influence the reward structure of the university.

Concerning the faculty development in academic planning project, it is now believed that before the Kellogg project there should have been a program to orient department chairmen more thoroughly to the management planning program. Although departments were accustomed to doing an annual SWOTs analysis, they had not progressed much further in implementing the management program when the Kellogg project began. Yet the Kellogg project required faculty to go beyond this point in their planning for Kellogg activites. Furthermore, out of fifty-nine planning activities, only four were divisional level projects, and only six were institutional level projects. Although the steering committee recognized this problem early and instructed the project directors to encourage faculty members to propose planning activities at the divisional and institutional levels, these efforts were not notably successful. It now appears that it would have been wiser to have the steering committee, or some other representative group of faculty, conduct a needs assessment and assign specific divisional and institutional level problems to task forces. Such an approach might also have led to a more productive use of the colloquia. Although the steering committee planned these programs according to its perceptions of important institutional issues, they were not always followed by related planning activities, which was their original purpose. Despite these problems, the W. K. Kellogg Foundation project "Faculty Development in Academic Planning: An Approach to Institutional Self-Renewal," which built upon earlier work done in management planning, made it possible for the Furman faculty to develop the skills necessary for effective academic planning and to use these skills in developing some exciting and innovative education programs. In addition, an unintended outcome was that potential faculty leaders were identified and given high visibility through project activities.

Conclusion

Planned change as a part of institutional renewal can lead to the achievement of desired results in colleges and universities. It is a move, however, toward decentralized, participative planning that can present some difficulties. But despite the difficulties, the participative style of planning and management holds tremendous promise. Problems will arise in a systematic approach to planned change, but the potential is great and the risks less than the other major options available to college and university administrators and faculty at the present time.

Has planned change been a reality at Furman University? Change has certainly occurred and is still occurring. It is believed that the changes have been deliberate, reasoned, and positive, and that the funded projects have contributed greatly to the success and quality of the changes.

Philip C. Winstead is coordinator of Institutional Planning and Research and professor of education at Furman University. He was codirector of the W. K. Kellogg-sponsored project, Faculty Development in Academic Planning: An Approach to Institutional Renewal, and is presently director of Programs for Faculty Development at Furman.

The involvement of large numbers of people in task groups,
organized and synthesized by a top-level leadership team,
characterized Wichita State University's approach to
leadership and management development.

Case Study:
The Wichita State University
Experience

David R. Alexander

The pressures faced by higher education today are especially challeng-
ing at Wichita State University where dramatic enrollment increases,
initiated when the institution entered the state system in 1964, were not
accompanied immediately by commensurate increases in physical
resources. Wichita State is one of six state supported universities in
Kansas, coordinated by the state board of regents. Sixteen thousand
students are enrolled in degree programs in six colleges, with degree
programs ranging from the associate degree level through two doctoral
degree offerings. Most of the students reside in the Wichita metropoli-
tan area, which has a population of a third of a million people. These
students are often older than traditional college age, working, and usually do not enroll for a full load of courses. As a result, the programs of
Wichita State must be especially responsive to the needs of the community and the surrounding region. Recognizing the need, the difficulties, and the challenge of evolving more appropriate management,
which would in turn provide for the maintenance of responsive, quality

G. Hipps (Ed.). *New Directions for Institutional Research: Effective Planned Change Strategies*, no. 33.
San Francisco: Jossey-Bass, March 1982.

programs in a period of declining enrollment, Wichita State University, with the support of the W. K. Kellogg Foundation, initiated a leadership and management development project.

Early in the development of the proposal to the Kellogg Foundation, two key issues were identified. First, if the project was to have a real impact on the management of the university, it would have to involve a sizeable percentage of the university community in developing activities. In order to organize and synthesize the activities of the various groups, an authoritative and highly visible leadership team was formed. Second, such a diverse project would require reasonably specific goals and objectives if the results and conclusions of the various groups were expected to address a common set of issues. Thus, not only did the original proposal specify the overall goals and objectives of the project, but also the first charge to each task force was to develop a set of goals for review by the leadership team at the end of phase I of the project.

Role of the Leadership Team. The concept of a leadership team was included in the project to serve several functions. For a broadly diversified project such as this, strong central coordination was required to prevent fragmentation into meaninglessness. While day-to-day coordination and administration was provided by a project director, decisions pertaining to the objectives of the project and to the future functioning of the institution required a broader base of participation. Furthermore, the ten members of the leadership team gave much needed visibility and respectability to the project. If large numbers of faculty and administrators were to be expected to devote significant time and energy to change some of the basic functional processes of the university, they would need the confidence that their conclusions would be heard and acted upon. The involvement of the highest levels of administration on campus on the leadership team was one important means of demonstrating this commitment. Finally, the concept of a leadership team provided a vehicle for developing the new approaches and abilities appropriate to steady state management. Their activities were designed to develop team members' analytical and problem solving skills and their capacity to function as a team.

Goals and Objectives of Project. An analysis of the strengths and needs of Wichita State led to the formulation of two basic goals and five objectives for the project. The two basic goals were: (1) to improve the university's ability to plan and manage change in order to meet steady state conditions, declining conditions, or new opportunities and (2) to respond to the needs for nontraditional approaches in higher education while preserving the strengths of the traditional. The five specific objectives of the project focused generally on the development of leadership abilities and on the specific areas of institutional planning, communication, faculty development, and administrative development.

Organization of Project Activities. The first year of the project, phase I, was devoted to identifying issues surrounding each of the objectives and to planning the approach to address those issues during phase II of the project. Four task forces were formed to study approaches to the four focus issues of the project. During phase II, the planning task force formed two new task forces in academic program planning and in program review and evaluation.

Development of the Mission and Strategies-for-the-Future Statement

The development of the mission and strategies-for-the-future statement was one of the major activities of the leadership team. The purposes for developing this statement were:

- To identify and facilitate creative and appropriate responses by the institution to changing conditions in higher education
- To reaffirm those things the institution does well, values highly, and wants to maintain at a quality level
- To interpret with greater specificity the meaning of mission statements prepared by external governing bodies
- To help identify and articulate the institution's role and aspirations to external publics to generate understanding and support
- To serve as a guide and framework for future decisions about programs and resources
- To provide a framework within which the colleges and departments can develop their own specific goals and plans.

If a mission and goals statement is to be useful as a planning document, all constituencies must have an opportunity to influence its development; key administrators must support it so that it will carry the weight of decision; and it must be sufficiently specific to allow the institution to anticipate the circumstances of the future. The first section of the statement that evolved specifically defines the "urban role" of the university as a part of its emerging character as a comprehensive regional university. The second section specifies directions for development in the areas of students and student life, educational programs, research, service, faculty, resources, and university governance and administration. Each of these areas is introduced by a statement of general purpose and followed by several statements of objectives and strategies.

Over 350 copies of a working draft of the mission statement were distributed. Written responses to the draft were requested from various constituencies of the university and from twenty national leaders in higher education. The leadership team met with various groups to discuss their reactions and suggestions. Because the special circumstances within each college may significantly affect institutional objectives, each college or other major unit also prepared a statement of its mission and goals after the university's statement had been distributed.

Improving Communication to Improve Management

The task force on communication was formed to strengthen internal and external communication in order to create an environment in which change of all kinds is articulated and discussed internally and the mission of the institution is clarified and advanced externally. The exploration of the topic of communication led the task force into areas of management, leadership, organizational structure, and institutional governance.

For purposes of study, the topic was divided into internal and external communication. Internal communication included all of the processes by which the institution communicates with its immediate organizational members: faculty, staff, and administrators. External audiences were the immediate urban population, the state-wide population, and specially identified opinion leaders or communicators (that is, media representatives, legislators, and community leaders). Students were considered external constituents. External communication included all of the processes by which the institution communicated with external audiences.

Internal Communication. During phase I of the project, the task force studied a number of different methods for investigating the nature of internal communication. One problem was inherent in most of the immediately available approaches: Could the task force conduct a study using people within the institution as resources for studying the institution? The solution was to seek assistance through the use of a communication audit research design offered by members of the International Communication Association (ICA), outside professionals who were experienced, credible, and free from bias (Goldhaber, 1976). A separate communication audit liaison committee was established to coordinate the ICA audit and to interpret the results to the university community. The purposes identified for the audit were: to describe individual, group, and organizational patterns of actual communication behaviors in terms of sources, channels, topics, and length and quality of interactions; to evaluate the quality of information communicated by various sources; to assess the quality of communication relationships; to identify common positive and negative communication experiences; and to provide general recommendations for change.

The ICA communication audit method as adapted for use at the university used four data gathering tools: a network analysis that requested the participants to indicate with whom they communicated on a regular basis within the organization; an attitude questionnaire that revealed attitudes toward communication practices and policies; a communication experiences form of briefly written examples of communication experiences; and an interview guide for use in individual interviews of key communicators and general faculty and staff. Over 1,000 of the faculty and staff, or 76 percent, responded to the first three forms. In addition, 123 people were interviewed in two-hour individual sessions by the team professionals who came to the campus to conduct the audit.

The use of a research data base for preparing recommendations for improving communication processes made those recommendations much easier to justify and implement. Although a number of strengths in communication were identified, some problems were noted such as the need to develop more fully the formal communication structure; to have formal communication policies; to reduce the ambiguity people have about their roles; to have more liaison or linking persons, especially horizontally; and to alleviate overload and response problems in several administrative areas.

External Communication. The identification of the important external public groups and the relevant communication issues for each group was the first priority for the task force as it began its consideration of external communication during phase I. Three of the identified external public groups were surveyed by the task force during phase II.

Mail-back questionnaires were distributed to a sample of students and to a sample of residents in the immediate urban area. The response rate to the mail-back questionnaires was low. The results, therefore, were somewhat ambiguous but some useful information was obtained.

The understanding and appreciation of the institution's function or nature by journalists is critical to determining the public's view of the institution. Recognizing this fact, the task force interviewed seven representatives of the news media. The interviews afforded an excellent opportunity to assess the quality of this critical external communication link and to discuss the university's point of view toward media coverage.

The major conclusion of these investigations was that the institution tended to take external communication for granted. The result was a frequent lack of coordination, confusing or misinformation, lack of information to the right audiences at the right time, and a generally imprecise public view of the university. In addition to twenty-seven specific recommendations for improving the communication process, the major recommendation of the task force was that the university needed a director of university relations. Such a person was needed to coordinate the implementation of the numerous specific recommendations of the task force as well as to provide coherence to both internal and external communication.

Planning for the Future:
The Development of a Planning Process

Because effective management of colleges and universities requires that decisions be directed toward the future and based on the experiences of the past, the development of a comprehensive planning and information system was identified as one of the five objectives of the project at Wichita State University.

During phase 1 of the project, a small task force was appointed by the leadership team to study how a planning process should be developed. The recommendations of the phase I task force divided the phase II activities into four areas: development of a comprehensive model for planning, study of existing and proposed program review procedures, integration of the six major university data banks, and improved coordination of both continuing and special institutional studies.

After considerable background study of planning activities and theory, a consensus developed surrounding the prerequisites for successful planning at WSU (compare, Kieft and others, 1978; Moore, 1976). First, a planning process could not replace the existing decision-making processes of the university. Second, a successful planning process had to be incorporated into the administrative structure as a regular, continuing activity. Third, if the planning effort was to be taken seriously by those asked to participate, the results had to be useful and used. Finally, planning activities had to have the visible support and active participation of the president. Three purposes for planning were identified for the university: (1) the establishment and review of goals and objectives for the university and its departments that are achievable and adaptable to changing conditions, (2) the coordination of broad-based and routine planning and review among the units of the university, and (3) the effective allocation of resources in a time of relatively stable budgets and enrollments. To accomplish these goals, a detailed ten-step planning process was developed. Key elements of the process included development of university and college planning assumptions, preparation of planning statements by departments, and frequent review and feedback concerning the results of the planning process.

When this recommendation was presented to the leadership team, it was determined to be too ambitious because of the time demands of the other project-related activities and because it was not sufficiently integrated with the line structure of the institution. As a result, a streamlined version of the process was proposed that more closely conformed to the line structure of the university and that emphasized communication rather than process. The activities included: (1) distribution of planning information, including discussion of the rationale of planning, departmental and institutional data, and specific planning questions; (2) preparation of departmental planning reports; (3) preparation of college planning summaries; (4) individual discussion of each college's planning issues with the president and academic vice-president; and (5) distribution and discussion of planning recommendations.

During the first cycle, education played a major role. Many faculty and administrators were not sympathetic to planning efforts, and many of the activities were unfamiliar. Individualized coordination and consultation were provided by two institutional planning coordinators and planning resource persons in each college. These persons met individually with departments, groups of chairpersons, and individual administrators to clarify the purposes of the planning process, to raise pertinent planning issues, and to provide planning information. The coordinators and planning resource persons also met frequently to identify and correct deficiencies in the planning process and to facilitate linkages among different units.

The primary outcome of the first cycle of the process was a greatly improved focus on institutional and college planning issues. Discussion of the issues at all levels within the institution has led to more rational decision processes with greater communication among affected parties. The second cycle built directly on the identification of issues to develop alternatives and priorities.

Quality Assurance Through
Program Review and Evaluation

At institutions in which budgets and enrollments are stable but demands upon programs are sometimes dramatically shifting, it is difficult but important to monitor academic quality. The initial activities of the program review and evaluation included discussing the philosophical questions of the content and objectives of program review and deciding who should be responsible for the quality of academic programs. An inventory of all existing program review activities at Wichita State, both external and internal, was performed.

It was recognized that program review and evaluation must serve a dual purpose at the university. For each academic program, self-study is a process necessary to ensure the maintenance and continued improvement of standards. For the university as a whole, program review enables faculty and administrators to ensure quality curricula, to provide for both student and faculty needs, and to facilitate the development of an effective relationship between resource allocation and the maintenance of academic excellence.

The major objective of the program review process is to identify and build on present strengths and to discover significant unmet needs of a program in terms of present requirements as well as justifiable aspirations. The process should lead to recommendations that request specific actions. The reviews also should be program reviews, although all programs within a department should be reviewed concurrently. Only academic departments were included initially, but inclusion of nonacademic units is anticipated in the future.

The review process contains three major components: self-study reports, review teams, and a university committee on program review and evaluation. The self-study report is prepared by the department undergoing review. Detailed guidelines for the preparation of this report are provided that attempt to focus attention on issues and prospects rather than statistics and past history. The review team consists of four or five faculty of the university. When appropriate, an external consultant also may be a member of the team. Specific guidelines for the review teams allow faculty with no previous exposure to the process to function effectively on the team. The role of the review team is to determine the accuracy and completeness of the self-study report but to make no recommendations for future decisions. This task was left to the university committee on program review and evaluation, which evaluates all programs on the basis of the self-study reports, review team reports, and other available documents. The dean and academic vice-president are included in the final stages of the evaluation so that they will be fully aware of the rationale for the recommendations and will have an opportunity to indicate the commitments the institution can make to carry out the recommendations. This review process operates on a five-year cycle for all programs.

Administrative Development for Effective Leadership

As institutions of higher education begin to deal with new issues such as restriction of resources, identification of nontraditional student markets, and the increasing need for accountability, new administrative skills and procedures will be required. The administrative internship program, ongoing administrative development, and administrative performance review were programs designed to meet these new requirements.

The Administrative Internship Program. The goals of the administrative internship program were:

- To introduce interns to administration as background for personal career decisions
- To assist selected faculty in developing the qualifications necessary for assuming administrative roles
- To provide a formal program through which the administrative abilities of women and minorities could be developed
- To create a faculty base of information about administration
- To encourage a dialogue that would permit interns to express to mentors their views as faculty members.

Each intern was selected primarily on the basis of individual needs and potential, with only secondary consideration given to the institutional benefits. Interns received a teaching load reduction of one third for one year.

An individual program of activities was designed to respond to the objectives and needs of each intern. Interns worked directly with a mentor in a high administrative position. A schedule of coordinated readings, seminars, and weekly evaluation meetings was monitored by the internship coordinator. The major disadvantages of this approach to administrative development are its expense and the inconvenience to the faculty member's department. Continuation of the program has been on a less formal basis, with greater emphasis on alternative means for accomplishing the same goals in less costly ways.

Ongoing Administrative Development Program. Because many university administrators have little or no formal training in administration, the development of specific management skills of current administrators is important if the institution is to adapt successfully to change. In order to study the process of organizational development and to initiate the planning activities necessary for the implementation of a specific program of administrative development, a series of workshops was held for central administrators and deans, assistant and associate deans, chairpersons, graduate coordinators, and classified personnel. Each workshop was planned by a small committee of the participants, with only general coordination from the task force. Among the issues discussed at these workshops were: changes in state funding processes, the role of assistant and associate deans in achieving institutional goals, the role of chairpersons in the administrative process, and personnel policies and procedures.

A combined workshop for all the previously involved administrators was held to share the results of the individual workshops and identify strategies for meeting continuing development needs for each group. Several recommendations were made by the task force following the completion of these activities, but the major conclusion was that a professional development center was needed to initiate and coordinate the ongoing development needs of administrators. It was anticipated that an overall plan of administrative development activities, involving all administrators, would be formulated based on an assessment of individual and institutional needs.

Administrative Performance Review. In recognition of the ways in which evaluation can contribute to development activities, the task force also initiated the design of a process for evaluating administrators. Extensive use was made of the existing literature on evaluation, both in an academic and in an industrial context, and of consultants both on and off campus. The specific issues addressed included which administrators were to be evaluated, who would initiate and make the evaluations, and the uses that would be made of the results.

The task force recommended that formal performance reviews be conducted on a regular three- to five-year cycle for all administrators down to the level of assistant dean. The review is summarized to include: (1) A discussion of previous goals, responsibilities, and tasks, their level of attainment, and difficulties encountered; (2) general goals, responsibilities, and tasks to be used in the next performance review; (3) a sample of the opinions of internal and external constituents relative to the administrator's performance; and (4) an assessment, made by an administrator's supervisor, of his or her strengths followed by suggestions for professional growth and by an agreement on the level of institutional support available for activities related to professional development.

Increasing Institutional Vitality Through Faculty Development

Changing demands on faculty, coupled with a reduction in faculty mobility, can jeopardize the ability of the institution to respond adequately to emerging concerns unless current faculty are encouraged and allowed to develop new skills and explore new approaches to their work. Two conditions are necessary for effective faculty development to occur in any educational institution. First, the faculty must recognize a need for development and take the initiative to seek and use the resources that are available. Second, the institution must provide such resources to motivate the faculty and create an atmosphere in which development is not only recognized as a primary goal but is actively encouraged.

The objectives of a faculty development program should be to encourage the growth of each faculty member in accordance with his or her strengths, deficiencies, and defined institutional role; and to enhance the performance level of the faculty as a group. To accomplish these objectives, an institution needs a development program that is comprehensive, well coordinated throughout the institution, respected by all faculty, visible in all institutional activities, and funded and staffed at a realistic level.

After the background study of the needs for and approaches to faculty development during phase I, it was considered important to broaden the base of faculty involvement in the design of the program itself. The original task force was enlarged to twelve members, and four committees were selected to assist the task force. Each of the committees had primary responsibility in a specific area: instruction, scholarly and creative activities, service, and personal-professional development. The task force then worked with the committees to formulate guidelines and procedures to bring about a holistic approach to faculty development.

The primary role of the committees was to identify current

development activities in their respective areas at Wichita State, to identify problems or impediments to faculty development, and to recommend a priority listing of activities that should be undertaken. The task force then combined and refined the lists of activities, developed a new order of priorities, estimated the cost and feasibility of the activities, and developed implementation guidelines for selected activities.

The major recommendation of the task force was that a faculty development center should be created to provide the necessary coordination and the appropriate visibility for the program. The staff of the center was to be responsible for identifying resource persons among the faculty, collecting resource materials, distributing information, and assisting faculty in using the resources available for professional and personal development.

After considering this recommendation, and a similar recommendation from the administrative development task force, the leadership team decided to establish a professional development center that encompasses faculty development in teaching, scholarly and creative activities, service, and personal-professional development and has an equal concern for administrative development. The center has a full-time coordinator, an equivalent full-time position to provide for release time for faculty to serve the center, and funds for honoraria for external consultants, secretarial support, and a small grants program.

Conclusion

The leadership and management development project has led to a number of significant changes at Wichita State University. An external evaluation of the project was provided by Formative Evaluation Research Associates both during the project and in a final evaluation report submitted by John A. Seeley (1978) at the conclusion of the project. As an institutional change model, the project had several important characteristics (Ahlberg, 1979). These include:

- The involvement of a larger number of faculty and staff in discussing a broad range of issues of importance to the institution
- The willingness to take the risks involved in addressing so many important issues simultaneously
- The involvement of the institution's top leadership in the leadership team
- The progressive inclusion of additional faculty and administrators

- The vertical integration of activities
- The development of a future orientation at all administrative levels.

Several facets of the project could be improved in future activities. For example:

- Horizontal communication among task forces was irregular and often resulted in insufficient coordination
- Many people were exhausted by the intensity and breadth of the project
- The accumulation of task force recommendations at the end of the project did not allow sufficient time for their consideration and timely implementation
- Some task forces were not provided sufficient direction from the institution's top leaders early in their deliberations.

Intangible results are hard to measure, but one of the most significant results has been the large number of faculty and administrators who now more clearly perceive the issues and problems that confront the university and are convinced that the activities we are and will be undertaking will benefit the institution. The pressures that have been generated to proceed with change are substantial and continuing.

Two years after the conclusion of the project, very few of the activities that were initiated during the project are being referred to as "Kellogg activities" although they continue to be important components of the institution. The professional development center is now an active and accepted part of the institution. The planning and program review processes have been incorporated into the functions of existing institutional offices.

Although this integration of project activities was the desired result of two years of coordinated implementation activities, the attitudes and abilities developed during the project have not disappeared. Routine internal and external communication processes continue to receive conscious attention from many people. The approach to emerging administrative and academic issues and opportunities continues to reflect the orientation and abilities developed during the project. It is in this sense that planned change has become an ongoing and evolving process at Wichita State University.

References

Ahlberg, C. G. "The Leadership and Management Development Project at Wichita State University." Paper presented at the American Association of State Colleges and Universities Conference, San Francisco, November 20, 1978.

114

Goldhaber, G. M. "The ICA Communication Audit: Rationale and Development." Paper presented at the Academy of Management Convention, Kansas City, August, 1976.

Kieft, R. N., Armijo, F., and Bucklew, N. S. *A Handbook for Institutional Academic and Program Planning: From Idea to Implementation.* Boulder, Colo.: National Center for Higher Education Management Systems, 1978.

Moore, J. W. "Pragmatic Considerations in Academic Planning." *Planning for Higher Education,* 1976, *5* (6), 3–5.

Seeley, J. A. *Leadership and Management Development Project at Wichita State University: Summary Evaluation Report.* Ann Arbor, Mich.: Formative Evaluation Research Associates, 1978.

David R. Alexander, associate professor of physics at Wichita State University, Kansas, served as coordinator of Kellogg Activities. In this role, he was responsible for coordinating the implementation of programs developed during the leadership and management development project and for disseminating the results of the project to other institutions.

The institutions represented in this volume have tested certain
processes and techniques that can be successfully implemented
in various types of colleges and universities.

Summary and Conclusions

G. Melvin Hipps

The University of Akron, Furman University, and Wichita State University vary greatly with regard to their history, their environment, their clientele, and their mission. They demonstrate the problems and the opportunities common to both rural and urban, large and small, new and old, public and private institutions. Thus, although they do not claim, either individually or collectively, to have developed a model for planned change that is transportable to another institution, they have tested certain processes and techniques that can be successfully implemented in various types of colleges and universities. The model for change that might be derived from these three programs, though it might not be transportable, can be generalized in such a way as to be relevant in other settings.

Figure 1 illustrates the common goals, the common elements, the individual approaches, and the individual characteristics of the three universities. Through their individual projects, each school was attempting to develop a model for institutional renewal and change and to design organizational structures and patterns necessary for renewal and change.

G. Hipps (Ed.). *New Directions for Institutional Research: Effective Planned Change Strategies,* no. 33.
San Francisco: Jossey-Bass, March 1982.

Figure 1

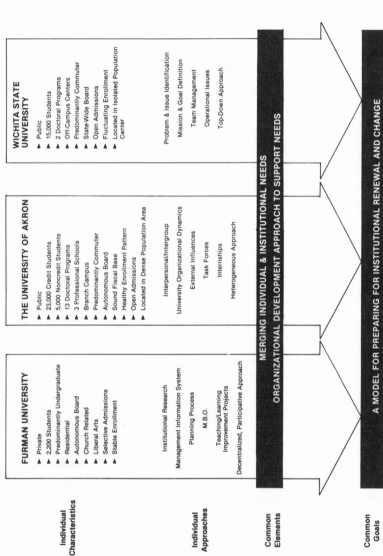

Individual Characteristics

FURMAN UNIVERSITY
- Private
- 2,200 Students
- Predominantly Undergraduate
- Residential
- Autonomous Board
- Church Related
- Liberal Arts
- Selective Admissions
- Stable Enrollment

THE UNIVERSITY OF AKRON
- Public
- 23,000 Credit Students
- 5,000 Noncredit Students
- 13 Doctoral Programs
- 3 Professional Schools
- Branch Campus
- Predominantly Commuter
- Autonomous Board
- Sound Fiscal Base
- Healthy Enrollment Pattern
- Open Admissions
- Located in Dense Population Area

WICHITA STATE UNIVERSITY
- Public
- 15,000 Students
- 2 Doctoral Programs
- Off-Campus Centers
- Predominantly Commuter
- State-Wide Board
- Open Admissions
- Fluctuating Enrollment
- Located in Isolated Population Center

Individual Approaches

Institutional Research
Management Information System
Planning Process
M.B.O.
Teaching/Learning Improvement Projects
Decentralized, Participative Approach

Interpersonal/Intergroup
University Organizational Dynamics
External Influences
Task Forces
Internships
Heterogeneous Approach

Problem & Issue Identification
Mission & Goal Definition
Team Management
Operational Issues
Top-Down Approach

Common Elements

MERGING INDIVIDUAL & INSTITUTIONAL NEEDS
ORGANIZATIONAL DEVELOPMENT APPROACH TO SUPPORT NEEDS

Common Goals

A MODEL FOR PREPARING FOR INSTITUTIONAL RENEWAL AND CHANGE

Characteristics of the Three Programs

The University of Akron sought to bring about renewal and change by involving a broad cross section of the administration, faculty, and staff in activities designed to develop leadership potential, to enhance interpersonal relationships, and to build a repertory of skills necessary for effective problem solving by groups. Another thrust of the program was to have participants engaged in a thorough study of organizational dynamics in colleges and universities and of trends and issues in higher education. The culmination of all of these activities was the establishment of task forces and administrative internships with the purpose to bring the new knowledge and skills of a rather larger percentage of the university community to bear in searching for solutions to problems faced by the institution. However, as important as solving particular problems might have been, the central purpose of the project at The University of Akron was to launch a new approach to organizational development based on providing the skill, knowledge, structures, and climate necessary for a large group of faculty, administration, and staff to work together in defining the mission of the institution and solving whatever problems might arise in the future. The focus of the project was neither the top nor the bottom of the university hierarchy. Furthermore, although the project had strong administrative backing, the impetus for the particular direction taken by the project came neither from the top nor the bottom. All levels and all segments of the university were simultaneously the focus of the project and provided the impetus for its direction.

The program for planned change and renewal at Furman University was based on a version of management by objectives. The program was thus grounded in the theory of organizational development that holds that institutional renewal and change can best be managed when decision making is based on information provided by sound institutional research, appropriate involvement of all members of the organization, systematic planning, and clear policies and procedures. As a decentralized, participatory model for management, the impetus of the program theoretically moves upward in the institutional hierarchy. However, the installation of the program came about in a somewhat different fashion. It was first implemented in the administrative and business operations of the institution and was later tested in the process of academic planning. Although a unified management program was ultimately developed, the planning of the program was focused first on the administration and then on the faculty. However, the faculty, not the administration, was responsible for implementing the program in the academic area.

At Wichita State University, the program for planned change concentrated on defining the university mission and goals, identifying problems and issues, developing a participatory approach to problem solving, and improving various institutional operations. The impetus for the project came from the administration, and thus this project illustrates a "top-down" approach to the management of change. The approach was to engage a leadership team (primarily administrators, since they tend to be in a position to take the larger view of institutional affairs) in identifying problems that needed to be solved, in structuring groups to research and suggest solutions to problems, and in implementing and evaluating courses of action. Assisting the leadership team were four task forces and numerous subcommittees. The problems addressed in this project focused on both operational issues (for example, communication, planning, program review, and so on) and personnel issues (for example, administrative review, faculty development, and so on).

Generalized Model for Change

It is obvious that the three universities differed in the specific structures and activities designed to bring about change. The program at The University of Akron concentrated on individuals and was thus based on the organizational theory that "a healthy person equals a healthy organization" and that an institution's goals can be advanced only when individuals perceive the relationship of these goals to their own interests. Essentially a management-by-objectives approach to managing change, the program at Furman University was based on a rational strategy. The program at Wichita State University was philosophically somewhere between those of Akron and Furman. Despite these differences, there are certain elements that were present in all three projects. These commonalities might reasonably be viewed as those elements the three universities believe to be essential for mounting a successful program for change. They therefore constitute whatever can be generalized from the three projects and used as guidelines by other institutions.

Definition of Institutional Mission. All three institutions initiated their change programs by developing mission statements. These statements resulted from lengthy and substantive debates among all constituents of the institutions and were sufficiently specific to leave no doubt about the nature of the schools, the particular clientele to be served, the kinds of needs to be met, and, by implication, the needs to be left unmet or left to other institutions. Without this kind of agreement on the nature and mission of an institution, there is no basis for a program of planned change. Furthermore, if a mission statement is so broad and general that it excludes nothing, then it is of questionable value in providing direction for efforts toward change and renewal. Each of the mission statements was constructed in the light of a thorough and honest analysis of the present and future environment of higher education in general and of the individual institution in particular.

Top Administrative Support. The programs at all three institutions had the unqualified support of top administrators, including the presidents. Furthermore, the chief executives were active participants in the programs and were thus highly visible. Although each program had capable leadership in the project directors or coordinators who were effective as change agents, these people could not have succeeded without the involvement of the presidents. Supporting a program designed to bring about change requires not only personal commitment on the part of top administration but also a willingness to take the risks which inevitably accompany such programs.

Leadership Development. Leadership development is probably the single most important component of all three programs. It is this fact that prompted the chapters on team leadership development and faculty and administrative development in this volume. Because of the emphasis on participatory decision making in each of the three programs, there was a recognition of the necessity to train individuals in the skills necessary for effective participation in the process. Both The University of Akron and Wichita State provided leadership internship programs; Akron also provided specific training in effective leadership of and membership in groups. Furman provided activities designed to enhance the abilities of faculty and administrators to engage in systematic planning and evaluation. Akron and Wichita approached problem solving through the work of task forces. Without education and training for these responsibilities, collaborative problem solving and decision making cannot become a reality.

Comprehensive Change Programs. The change programs at all three universities were comprehensive in nature. Effective programs of this sort cannot be piecemeal. There must be recognition that change in one area' affects many other areas; therefore, a planned change effort must involve all systems, all operations, and all personnel. The particular projects supported by the W. K. Kellogg Foundation were only a part of the broad institutional programs designed to bring about change. For example, the team leadership program at The University of Akron was only a part of a total change program coordinated by the commission on institutional planning and development. The project on faculty development in academic planning at Furman University was one aspect of the institutional management planning program that was developed over the entire decade of the 1970s. The project on leadership and management development at Wichita State University was part of a broad program that ultimately brought all institutional operations under scrutiny and effected change in all of these operations. These programs illustrate the fact that successful change efforts are not only comprehensive but also time consuming.

Colleges and universities that attempt to solve the problems of declining enrollments, inflation, shifts in the supply and demand in the labor market, and declining financial support by starting a continuing education program, dropping foreign language and installing a nursing program, or creating a development department — rather than by embarking on a total institutional program of planned change — may be setting the stage for more severe problems in the future.

The comprehensive nature of change programs at the three institutions illustrates a practice common to all three, that is, to seek external funding only for support of a portion of a total program that has been planned and that has the backing of all segments of the university community.

Participation. There was a recognition at all three institutions that one person or even a group of administrators cannot effectively control and direct all of the activities of a complex organization such as a college or university. Mounting a successful program of planned change, therefore, requires the commitment and participation of all members of the academic community. This approach to organizational development implies that the quality of decision making will be improved by the participation in the process by a wide cross section of the institutional personnel, and that people will be more likely to accept decisions that they have helped to make. All three programs illustrate the belief that effective change cannot be mandated from the administration. Although the process of change brought about by participatory management might be viewed as slow and tedious by some, it is the only approach that is likely to produce lasting results.

Emphasis on Communication. In one way or another, all three institutions emphasized the need for improved internal and external communication as a prerequisite to an effective change program. Furman University's management program rests upon an intricate network of communication through the constantly revised planning book and the policies and procedures manual. Wichita State University assigned a task force to the problem of improving communications, and a communications audit was subsequently conducted by an external group. The dialogue generated by the classes, forums, and task forces at The University of Akron demonstrated the centrality of communication among all levels of university operations if significant changes are to occur.

Emphasis on Process. Although the programs at the three universities addressed specific problems, their major emphasis was on developing a process by which the institution could deal effectively with the changes occurring rapidly in the environment of higher education. Furman's program emphasized the process of systematic planning. Akron's program stressed the process of leadership development and problem solving by groups. Wichita State's program tended to focus more on the processes involved in the problems being addressed (that is, communications, institutional planning, and program evaluation) than on the organizational process (group dynamics, interpersonal relations, and participatory management) employed to address the problems; but because new organizational processes were employed in studying the problems, they have had great influence on the process of decision making.

Merging of Individual and Institutional Goals. Each of the three projects emphasize the importance of merging individual and institutional needs and goals. The values, attitudes, beliefs, and aspirations of every member of the academic community must be taken into account in any effective effort to bring about change because meaningful change in behavior comes about only as a result of changes in the attitudes, values, and beliefs of individuals. Furthermore, if colleges and universities are to survive the challenges of the next decades, each member of the academic community must view his own interests and aspirations as inextricably bound up in the mission and goals of the institution of which he or she is a part. Raising the level of consciousness of the faculty, administration, and staff about this situation must be a priority in any program designed to bring about change.

The elements that are common to the three change projects are obviously not meant to provide a "blueprint" for such projects, but guidelines for those who may be involved in or planning to initiate programs of this sort. Officials at all three schools have admitted that it is too early to evaluate the results of these programs. Since people were the object of the change effort in all three programs, it is difficult to measure the change that has occurred as a result of the programs. One can only judge the extent to which the structures are maintained that were created to involve individuals in decision making and to develop the skills necessary for participation in institutional governance.

No one can predict the future with certainty, but The University of Akron, Furman University, and Wichita State University are facing the future with more confidence than would have been possible without their programs for planned change. These schools have developed climates, structures, and processes that allow them not only to solve the problems of the present but to anticipate the challenges of the future. The three schools hope their experiences can be of some benefit to other schools that are attempting to manage the forces of change at work in them. The University of Akron, Furman University, and Wichita State University are grateful to the W. K. Kellogg Foundation not only for its support in their individual projects but also for making it possible for them to share their experiences with others laboring in higher education.

G. Melvin Hipps, currently a writer and consultant in higher education, was formerly professor of education and English, associate academic dean, chairman, Department of Education, director of Graduate Studies, and coordinator of Programs for Faculty Development at Furman University. He was codirector of the Kellogg project at Furman.

*The three institutions in this study are still in the process of
testing whether or not these new approaches to planned change
will lead to new programs and educational strategies for
implementing their new missions and for dealing with their
current and future student clientele.*

An Outsider's View:
Prelude, Interlude, or Postlude

Marvin W. Peterson

In presenting an epilogue, it is fair to point out that this author is an
"outsider" only in a technical sense. I was not a member of the three
institutions involved in these Kellogg-sponsored projects and had no
direct role in any of them. However, my involvement in a number of
the project activities at each of these three institutions, combined with a
personal interest in their planning and change strategies, provides me
with more than an academic "outside" perspective. Rather, it provides
a perspective and an awareness of some of the personalities involved, a
more intimate sense of the day-to-day challenges faced by these projects, and a better sense of the institutional dynamics with which they
interacted. These are important dimensions of any change process that
are difficult to convey in case studies—particularly those written by the
project directors—and perspectives that I hope will enrich this epilogue.

The Common Purpose: Prelude, Interlude, or Postlude

Examining the experiences of these three institutions, one is
torn between viewing these institutional efforts at planned change with

G. Hipps (Ed.). *New Directions for Institutional Research: Effective Planned Change Strategies*, no. 33.
San Francisco: Jossey-Bass, March 1982.

confident anticipation about their future impact, with hopeful uncertainty, or with deserved satisfaction with their results to date. Whatever view one might take, it is now time to reflect upon the inevitable transition period from the excitement of introducing a new order to the more mundane, ongoing institutionalization of new processes and activities. These three institutions planned change strategies to successfully introduce in each institution a comprehensive array of new approaches to planning, management, communication, information and analysis, and staff development. However, they are still in the process of testing whether or not these new approaches will lead to new programs and new educational strategies for implementing their new missions and for dealing with their current and future student clientele. Viewing the larger purposes of these planned change activities — educational change and institutional vitality — raises a dilemma. Can we anticipate that these institutions' accomplishments to date are a prelude to real renewal and change in their educational missions and programs, an interlude between current accomplishment and the real challenge ahead, or a postlude to successful planned change that introduced new ways of doing business that may dissipate or not have the desired results as resources become more limited?

Supportive or Inhibiting Factors

In a historical sense the experience of these institutions in the context of organizational change in higher education makes the Akron, Furman, and Wichita experiences somewhat unique and heroic. Rudolph (1965) has suggested that, historically, higher education institutions, instead of planning for change, merely recognize after the fact that change has taken place. Most changes in higher education have been occasioned by the addition of new institutions; by the creation of systems of institutions; by a forceful leader or promises of new resources; or by the addition, deletion, merging, or differentiation of units brought about by some evolutionary change process or top-down mandate. Planned change efforts, in the sense that this book defines them, are usually applied only to very limited segments of an institution. The relative uniqueness of these institutions' experience — a comprehensive institutional change introduced in a planned change strategy — provides us with an opportunity to examine some interesting dimensions of change (Baldridge and Deal, 1975) in addition to those elements of the change process enumerated by Melvin Hipps in Chapter Eight.

Influence of External Environments. Increasingly, we are aware that extrainstitutional dimensions are significant features in successful change processes. During the late 1970s, when these three institutions were undertaking their planned change efforts, to this writer's knowledge, there were no substantial enrollment declines or financial cutbacks affecting the institutions, as was the case at some colleges and universities. Furman's reputation allowed it to attract resources and students. The location of Akron and Wichita, in major urban areas where they were the dominant institution with a traditional urban or regional role, shielded them from the enrollment declines of some other institutions.

All three institutions also benefit from an external governance system supportive of institutional planning. At Furman, a private institution, the board was involved and favorably inclined. The Ohio Board of Regents has strongly encouraged and even supported institutional-level planning to supplement state-level efforts. Although the Kansas Board of Regents has probably provided less direct support, they did mandate institutional-level planning. In neither state was there an apparent attempt to restrict or prevent the programs and changes being introduced. This supportive, or at least benign, environment allowed a relatively stable period in which to address the extensive planned change effort. These conditions may not continue but have been clearly advantageous to date. A major benefit to all three institutions, of course, has been the availability of external grant funds to underwrite many of the planned change process activities. While these raise transitional issues when they are discontinued, the institutions seem aware of them.

Planned Change and Governance. A key element in the long-term success of a planned change process is how the change process itself and its resultant new activities relate to the institutional governance structure. All three institutions were sensitive to the issue of either making the governance system a target of change and/or making their change process or new programs and activities "fit" the institutional pattern of decision making. Because the introduction of planning and a planned change process involves a certain rational process (mission, goals and objectives, needs assessment, problem solving, program development, evaluation, and feedback), it often conflicts with collegial (Millett, 1962, 1978), rigid bureaucratic (Stroup, 1966), political (Baldridge, 1971, 1978; Mortimer and McConnell, 1978), or even anarchic (Cohen and March, 1973) decision processes now widely described in the literature about governance in higher education. If the governance process does not implicitly become a target of the planned change process or if the process and its resulting new programs are not carefully linked to the governance process, there will be a poor "fit" that may undermine the change effort.

To an extent, these problems of "fit" were recognized in the case studies. Furman addressed the problem directly by making their governance or decision-making process a major target of the change effort by introducing a management-by-objectives system. At Akron, Buchtel mentions some of the problems addressed in the task force and the issues of moving from individual to organizational-level change to deal with frustrations of team development participants who could not quickly affect the larger institutional setting. Wichita recognizes the problem in Alexander's description by including administrative as well as faculty development as a major thrust of their effort. Of course, all three institutions structure their change efforts to involve administrators and members of key governance groups as a linkage feature, and all were concerned with structuring their resulting new programs in the best place in the administrative hierarchy or reporting relationship to governance groups.

Initiating Conditions and Institutional Readiness. A key element in a successful change process is the initiating conditions and organizational readiness to participate. All three of the institutions had favorable conditions and a reasonable degree of readiness. The supportive nature of the environment and the support by top administrators have already been described.

An important characteristic was a source of external funding that did more than merely provide for the effort on each campus. Because several institutions were involved, became linked early in the process, and are identified with a multiinstitutional effort, the institutions individually probably attained even greater visibility to reinforce the positive symbolic value of their individual grants from Kellogg and other sources. These rewards may have influenced the readiness of the institutions and many of their members to participate — or more importantly sustained them when difficulties arose.

Another important dimension in readiness is that each institution seemed to begin with a clear definition of a current self-perceived problem toward which the planned change effort would be directed, in addition to the more generic longer-term problems described in Christenson's chapter. At Akron, there was a concern about how to get an increased sense of commitment and sense of mission by staff and the need to strengthen second- and third-echelon staff in an institution with a traditionally strong presidential style. At Furman, anticipation of the impending enrollment and financial pressures on the private institutions provided the motivation to begin on this path in 1971 with grants from Ford and Exxon. Their current need grew out of the experience. At Wichita, the impetus for the change project was apparently a ten-year accreditation review that had been pursued seriously and had identified some specific weaknesses and areas needing to be addressed.

Thus, the initiating conditions—a supportive environment, a stable institutional period, a visible and externally funded effort, strong top administrative support, and a clear sense of institutional problems to be addressed—all suggest that, if there was not institutional readiness, there was in fact a favorable set of initiating conditions to launch the effort, ensuring initial commitment to sustain the planned change program.

Leadership and Planned Change. The element of leadership—not just the supportive top administration—but leadership of the planned change process, which the other authors have modestly downplayed, deserves mention. The staffs of the three projects were all respected faculty and/or administrators in their institutions with a history of active leadership. They possessed both practical and theoretical knowledge of the planned change professional's tool box: skills in organizational assessment and diagnosis, group dynamics, problem solving, education or training, and evaluation. What they did not possess, they reinforced through their judicious use of consultants and outside experts, internal experts, and their own willingness to learn.

Without getting involved in the time-worn debate over whether or not one can be an effective internal planned change agent, these individuals performed successfully. These three institutions had a set of internal leaders of the planned change effort who "fit" the role of an internal agent. That is a resource few institutions may have, and I doubt that an external agent could provide the sensitive and sustained leadership these three institutions have had that reinforces the potential of successful implementation of these activities.

Some Comments on the Change Process. This discussion has already focused on several elements of the planned change process, but a few other insights emerge from the case studies. In all of these institutions the targets, agents, strategy, and content of the planned change process were clearly defined. This may have been due in part to the clarity of specific institutional needs that these efforts were designed to address and the leadership cadre, but it is also clear that each institution took the time to plan the coordinating structure, the strategies, the specific activities, and resulting programs of its planned change process.

However, the planned change leadership group was also willing to learn and modify its initial strategies when appropriate. For example, when Wichita divided its planning and information systems task force into one on academic planning and one on program development, or when Akron decided to address the problem of moving individual change to a more effective organizational level, they were demonstrating their ability to adapt their plans to address unforeseen circumstances. Furman even designed into its program decision points to "opt out," thus treating the planned change effort itself as an experiment. This opportunity to preplan and to learn and modify the process identifies an important ingredient in these three programs. Too often organizational change efforts in higher education n the past two decades have reflected hasty attempts to incorporate new approaches or techniques as solutions to current, and often superficially examined, problems — seeking a panacea rather than basic organizational change.

Higher educational institutions are justly criticized for poor management or inefficiency; they seize a tool, technique, or approach (such as PPBS, participatory democracy, simulation modeling, and so forth) from another setting (often business and government) without examining how well it worked there or whether it can work in their own institution; they introduce the approach without modification; and then become disenchanted and reject it or go through an agonizing reappraisal. These three institutions had enough time and the good sense to avoid that practice.

To the common process characteristics of the three programs identified by Hipps in Chapter Eight, I would add one more. I believe the case studies demonstrate an awareness of the need to integrate the new structures into the institutional administrative and governance structure and of the need to provide staff and resource support to the new program during and after the initial phases of development and as external funds are depleted. Whether the structural integration and longer term institutional resource commitment will be adequate or will, in fact, occur is not clear. However, all of these process characteristics suggest potential for fully integrating the new program and activities.

Conclusion

The external and internal context of these three institutions in launching their comprehensive planned change efforts may be as unique as the fact that they did it. The supportive external and environmental factors, the institutions' stability and readiness during this period, the concern for relating the planned change efforts to governance, the internal planned change leadership of the institutions, and the nature of the process all suggest a prelude to successful integration of the new activities and an opportunity to accomplish the larger common purpose — the achievement of their new or revised institutional mission and the reform or improvement of their educational activities to achieve it.

However, few institutions will have the conditions of stability and the array of supportive characteristics that these three were able to take advantage of to introduce a comprehensive planned change effort. As these three institutions and others interested in comprehensive, planned change face the difficult times that Christenson portrayed in the beginning of this book, four questions still remain.

1. Have Akron, Furman, and Wichita selected viable missions for the future *or* only the means for achieving some greater capacity to change and react?

2. Will their new programs and activities be sustained in terms of the resources and the individual and institutional commitment required when, and if, they face greater enrollment and financial strain?

3. Can their participatory, open, and rational planned change process be sustained in the potentially divisive, centralizing, and demoralizing conditions of severe resource decline? Or at least better than other approaches?

4. In the broader sense, can this process be introduced into less stable institutions or those already in a crisis?

My response to the first three is hopeful. The previous review suggests favorable conditions for integrating the new programs and processes — a *prelude* for Akron, Furman, and Wichita. Successful integration depends on the commitment of these institutions (their work is not done) to make this planned change effort work and on the environmental uncertainties ahead.

My answer to the fourth question is more cautious. Most other institutions will not share the supportive contextual, institutional, and professional staff features of these three institutions. However, in these three they can see the enthusiasm, commitment, and potential for institutional renewal and change. They can also see the most important lesson, namely, they remind us that there are no easy solutions to comprehensive organizational change. Even the planned change process has to be designed to meet the context, the needs and opportunities, and the strengths of their own institutions. Borrowed solutions — direct attempts to use the answers, programs, and activities of these three institutions — will not work. But the process of planned change and the experience of these three institutions identifies some concrete steps and a sensitivity to issues that do address the complexities of introducing significant organizational change. Other institutions considering a comprehensive change effort are at an *interlude*. They have had an opportunity to learn from Akron, Furman, and Wichita and to see the promise. But now they must assess their own need for such an effort, how it might be approached, and what resources and commitment it would require, and what it might accomplish.

Clearly, the answers to the four questions await future evaluation. These three institutions have given us an excellent set of pilot experiments and a basis for that evaluation and feedback. But isn't that part of the planned change process?

References

Baldridge, J. V., and others. *Policy Making and Effective Leadership: A National Study of Academic Management.* San Francisco: Jossey-Bass, 1978.

Baldridge, V. *Power and Conflict in the University.* New York: Wiley, 1971.

Baldridge, V. and Deal, T. *Managing Change in Educational Organizations.* Berkeley, Calif.: McCutchan, 1975.

Cohen, M. and March, J. *Leadership and Ambiguity.* New York: McGraw-Hill, 1973.

Millett, J. *The Academic Community.* New York: McGraw-Hill, 1962.

Millett, J. D. *New Structures of Campus Power: Success and Failures of Emerging Forms of Institutional Governance.* San Francisco: Jossey-Bass, 1978.

Mortimer, K., and McConnell, T. *Sharing Authority Effectively: Participation, Interaction, and Discretion.* San Francisco: Jossey-Bass, 1978.

Richman, B. M., and Farmer, R. N. *Leadership, Goals, and Power in Higher Education: A Contingency and Open-Systems Approach to Effective Management.* San Francisco: Jossey-Bass, 1974.

Rudolph, F. *The American College and University, A History.* New York: Vintage Books, 1965.

Stroup, H. *Bureaucracy in Higher Education.* New York: Free Press, 1966.

Marvin W. Peterson is professor of higher education and and director of the Center for the Study of Higher Education at the University of Michigan. He is editor-in-chief of New Directions for Institutional Research *and has served on the executive committees of the Association for Institutional Research, Association for the Study of Higher Education, and the Society for College and University Planning.*

Index